KU-196-520

Contents

Economic Growth with Equity

Lessons from East Asia

Kevin Watkins

Oxfam Publications

front cover photograph: Jakarta, Indonesia. J Hartley/Oxfam

Available from the following agents:
for Canada and the USA: Humanities Press International, 165 First Avenue, Atlantic
Highlands, New Jersey NJ 07716-1289, USA; tel. 732 872 1441; fax 732 872 0717
for Southern Africa: David Philip Publishers, PO Box 23408, Claremont, Cape Town 7735,
South Africa; tel. (021) 644136; fax (021) 643358
for Australia: Bush Books, PO Box 1370, Gosford South, NSW 2250, Australia;
tel. (043) 233274; fax (029) 212248
for the rest of the world contact: Oxfam Publishing, 274 Banbury Road, Oxford OX2 7DZ, UK

Published by Oxfam GB, 274 Banbury Road, Oxford OX2 7DZ

JB004/RB/98

Printed by Oxfam Print Unit

Oxfam GB is a registered charity no. 202918, and is a member of Oxfam International.

Preface

This *Insight* book started life as a short briefing paper prepared for the annual meeting of the International Monetary Fund (IMF) and the World Bank in Hong Kong in September 1997. The aim of the briefing paper was to draw attention to the success of East Asian countries in combining high growth with equity — and in achieving levels of poverty reduction which are without historical precedent. Shortly after the briefing paper went to print, the full extent of the financial crisis in East Asia began to emerge, as first Thailand and then Indonesia and South Korea were forced to turn to the IMF to avert outright collapse. Almost overnight, it seemed, the East Asian 'miracle' was being converted into a mirage, with the financial crisis spilling over into the real economy and threatening to reverse progress towards poverty reduction.

Pronouncements on the death of the East Asian 'miracle' are, in Oxfam's view, at best premature and at worst wildly misplaced. The foundations upon which the region's social and economic advance have been built remain intact, however severely they have been shaken. Social investment in basic health and education has created a stock of human capital which has been instrumental both in sustaining economic growth, and in converting growth into poverty reduction. At the same time, the redistribution of productive assets has enabled the poor in East Asia to produce their way out of poverty, creating a mutually reinforcing process of economic growth and social advance. Governments in Latin America and sub-Saharan Africa should, as we suggested in the original briefing paper, still be asking themselves why their economies have to grow at up to five times the rate of those in East Asia to achieve the same rate of poverty reduction.

This said, the financial crisis does pose an unprecedented challenge to East Asia and the wider international community. The economic mismanagement which contributed to the crisis is in large measure the product of corrupt, autocratic, and anachronistic political structures, under which government has become a vehicle for the pursuit of private vested interest. Banking systems and finance ministries have become conduits for the transfer of public funds to powerful but inefficient corporations, or, as in Indonesia, to the extended families of political leaders. For too long, governments in East Asia have maintained the myth that economic success and social advance are not consistent with a transition to more democratic political structures. The lesson of the present crisis is that they are not consistent with autocracy and unaccountability — and that political reforms are urgently needed to support economic reforms.

For the international community, the challenge is to develop a response to the financial crisis which protects the gains of the past, while supporting the reforms needed to maintain future progress. It is failing in this challenge. The failure is not in the speed or scale of resource mobilisation. Over $100bn has been committed to the region under IMF auspices since the crisis began, dwarfing the financial response to previous crises. The problem is that insufficient attention has been paid to the specific circumstances of East Asia. Conditions attached to IMF loans parallel those familiar from the Latin American debt crisis of the 1980s. They reflect a bias towards deflation and fiscal austerity which are not only inappropriate, given the underlying economic conditions, but which threaten to turn recession into a full-blown depression. Other conditions — such as the requirement that banking systems are opened up to foreign ownership — threaten to cause further instability, and appear to bear the heavy imprint of US influence and self-interest.

The text of the September 1997 briefing paper has been extended and updated to take into account the financial crisis and the response to it. The resulting *Insight* book, like the earlier paper, has benefited from discussions with and comments from a number of Oxfam colleagues, including Tony Burdon, Heather Grady (Vietnam), Siddo Deva, Lot Felizco (Philippines), Justin Forsyth, Jan Klugkist (Novib), Dianna Melrose, John Sayer, Veena Siddarth, Patrick Watt, and Lydia Williams (Oxfam US).

Finally, a word on 'East Asia'. In keeping with common usage, we use this term to refer to countries in the south-east of the region, as well as the east proper. Where regional data on poverty are used, the relevant countries are specified in the text.

Introduction

Twenty-five years ago Mei Hong's parents left their village in China's north-west province of Xianjing and moved to the southern town of Shenzhen. Like millions of families in the developing world, they were attempting to escape desperate rural poverty. Unlike most, they succeeded. Mei Hong now works in Shenzhen's special economic zone, one of the country's fast-expanding industrial areas. Life is hard, but living standards are far higher than those the family left behind — and they are rising fast.

Last year Mei Hong gave birth to her first child, Yu Lee — a name which means 'new hope'. The name is an apt description of what has happened to the poor in China. In 1972, when Yu Lee's grandparents were leaving Xianjing, one in three Chinese lived in poverty, unable to meet their basic needs for food, clothing, and shelter. Illiteracy was widespread and child mortality rates were high. Today, poverty afflicts less than one in ten Chinese. Child mortality has fallen by more than half, and fewer than 10 per cent of people between the ages of 10 and 25 are illiterate. Children like Yu Lee are twice as likely to reach their first birthday than children born to her grandparents' generation, and they will live on average ten years longer.

Yu Lee is the beneficiary of a revolution which has swept over East Asia in the past three decades. Built on the foundations of growth with equity, it is a revolution which resulted in the fastest reduction in poverty for the largest number of people ever witnessed in history — and it is a revolution which provides lessons for other regions. Complacency based upon past achievement is a luxury East Asia can ill afford. Yet in a world where one in three people live in a state of absolute want, and where the number of poor continues to rise, the region provides a beacon of hope in the midst of pervasive gloom, serving as a reminder that the war against poverty can be won. Encouraging as the achievements of the past may be, there are powerful obstacles to continued progress. The current financial crisis is one such obstacle. What started as a crisis in financial systems has now been transmitted to the real economy, undermining production and employment. Poverty levels are rising across the region, and there is now a real danger that the gains of the past will be reversed. Restoring stability while protecting these gains and maintaining the momentum towards poverty reduction poses a challenge to governments across the region. It also poses a challenge to the industrialised countries, which have mobilised resources for IMF-sponsored rescue packages with an apparent disregard for their impact on poverty. The World Bank has recently been drafted in to finance the creation of social welfare safety-nets, but, welcome as these are, they bear all the hallmarks of hastily contrived afterthoughts. What is needed is the integration of poverty-reduction considerations into the macro-economic reform measures adopted in response to the crisis.

Looking beyond the immediate crisis, there are problems to be confronted if progress in human development is to be maintained. Rising inequality is one such problem. Part of East Asia's success in poverty reduction has been built upon the equitable sharing of the benefits of economic growth, especially in comparison with other developing regions. During the 1990s, however, growth has been accompanied by a widening divide in income, with the gap between rich and poor becoming ever larger. There is also a huge 'democratic deficit'. Economic development has been pursued under governments which, for all their political differences, share in common a deep hostility to the principles of democracy and accountability. Moreover, the growth which has driven poverty reduction has been accompanied by extreme forms of exploitation — notably of female labour — and environmental destruction. In Mei Hong's home-town of Shenzhen, it has been estimated that one-half of all factories violate health and safety laws. Young women, driven to the city by extreme rural poverty, are required to work long hours in dangerous conditions, without even the most basic welfare protection. Industrial accidents are common, and trade union rights almost non-existent. Outside of the factories, public health is threatened by high levels of water and air pollution. The problems which children like Yu Lee will face as a result of these harsh realities are as significant as the opportunities they will have for a better life. This year, an estimated 178,000 people living in China's cities will suffer premature death because of pollution.[1] The mental development of children in major cities is threatened by blood-lead levels which average 80 per cent higher than those defined as dangerous by international standards.

Past successes and failures

This book examines some of the positive lessons for poverty reduction and growth to emerge from East Asia. It asks why the region has been so successful in comparison to other regions in combining high levels of growth with rapid progress towards poverty reduction. But the darker side of the East Asian miracle should not be forgotten. Poverty is about more than low incomes and social welfare indicators. It is also about an inability to exercise basic human and political rights, the absence of dignity, deprivation in knowledge and communication, environmental impoverishment, and the violation of the rights of women. In the international league table for poverty reduction, East Asia ranks at the top. On these broader indicators for human development it would rank far lower. For other developing regions, the challenge is to learn from East Asia's success in advancing social and economic welfare. The challenge for East Asia is to develop more participatory approaches to development, in which the poor are given a political stake in society as well as an economic and social stake.

There are other limits to the East Asian success story. While past achievements have been impressive, there are still 345 million people living below the World Bank poverty line of $1 a day.[2] In China there are 270 million people in poverty — more than in the whole of sub-Saharan Africa. Moreover, progress towards poverty reduction has not been uniform across the region. The Philippines has a lamentable record, with its share of the region's poor doubling over the past two decades. During the 1990s Vietnam has emerged as the latest high performer in the growth and poverty reduction league-tables, but it has a great deal of catching up to do. Along with Lao PDR, it is one of two countries in the region with over 40 per cent of the population in poverty — and the intensity of poverty is far greater than elsewhere in the region. In rural areas of Vietnam, the average income of the poor is 20 per cent below the poverty line.

Poverty in the region is to be found in its most concentrated form among small farmers, the landless, fishing communities, and indigenous or tribal communities, often living in geographically remote areas. Early in 1997, 2,000 people established a camp outside Government House in Bangkok. They were drawn from impoverished rural areas in the north-east of the country, from slums in Bangkok, from villages where communities had been displaced by large-scale development projects, and from trade unions. Within two weeks, the camp had grown to 20,000 people, and its residents, now organised into a Forum for the Poor, had outlined demands for a new pattern of development capable of responding to the needs of the marginalised.[3] As an expression of the failure of existing growth patterns to benefit the poor, the protest in Thailand was an element of a wider protest movement.

Across the region, rapid growth, with all of its benefits in terms of poverty reduction, has been achieved at a high price. Natural resource mismanagement has left a legacy of environmental destruction which has undermined the livelihoods of vulnerable communities. The power and infrastructure demands of industry have spawned huge projects, often financed by the World Bank and other multilateral donors, which have displaced millions of poor people, usually without adequate compensation. In urban areas, the presence of sprawling slums is testament to the uneven distribution of the benefits from growth. But it is in rural areas that poverty remains deepest and most pervasive. Alongside the poverty, islands of prosperity emerged to highlight the divide between rich and poor. Before the financial crisis struck, Thailand was one of the world's largest markets for Mercedes Benz cars. Yet in the rural north-east, poverty levels are of dimensions more familiar from Africa. Political protest in Thailand has been a response to the rapid increase in inequality which has accompanied high growth. Inequalities are also widening in other countries. The economically powerful in East Asia acquired all the trappings of Western consumerism, with imports of luxury goods flourishing. At the other end of the social scale are the poor who, lacking political power, are often treated appallingly. The relocation of urban squatters, the eviction of farmers from their land, the violation of indigenous land-rights in the interests of domestic and foreign investors, and the suppression of civil society are among the more visible outrages perpetrated against the poor. To add to these problems there are signs that economic growth is slowing, and with it, progress towards the eradication of poverty.

A 'miracle' under threat

Other clouds have appeared on the East Asian horizon over the past year. During the 1980s countries such as Malaysia, Thailand, and Indonesia followed the first generation of 'tiger economies' in combining breakneck economic growth-rates with financial stability. The region has, in many respects, reaped the benefits of globalisation. Rapid export growth has been one mechanism increasing the region's integration with the global economy — and export growth has been converted into high rates of job creation and rising real wages. East Asia is the only developing region to have consistently expanded its share of world trade over the past three decades. The region has also attracted a large proportion of the private capital flows which have surged in the 1990s. Over the past five years, it has absorbed more than 40 per cent of the private capital invested in developing countries. However, integration in the global economy creates risks as well as opportunities. The benefits of successful participation founded on good policies are high, but so too are the costs of policy mistakes. This is a lesson which East Asia is now learning, to its cost.

During 1997, the region's reputation for stability evaporated in a rolling cloud of financial turmoil, the effect of which has spread to Wall Street, to European stock markets, and to Latin America. Concern over 'contagion', or the spread of instability across global markets, has prompted the industrialised countries to contrive massive financial rescue packages, now totalling over $100bn, under the auspices of the International Monetary Fund (IMF).

Some commentators have been swift to pronounce the Asian miracle dead and buried, claiming that the currency crisis is a symptom of terminal economic problems.[4] The date on the tombstone reads 'July 1997', when Thailand's devaluation marked the onset of a regional financial crisis. Others have cited the latest crisis as evidence that there has been no miracle, but a mirage built on the foundations of inefficient state intervention.[5] Both arguments contain a germ of truth, in the midst of wild exaggerations. The hard fact is that no other group of countries in the developing world has sustained more rapid economic growth or achieved more dramatic poverty reduction. Contrary to the increasingly popular view, the miracle was not a mirage. Absolute poverty has been virtually eliminated in Korea, Malaysia, and Thailand; and Indonesia, which was a scattering of poverty-stricken islands 30 years ago, is in sight of the same goal. Of course, the challenge ahead remains formidable — and East Asia's economic growth rates have obscured serious structural shortcomings. But while the region's economies face systemic problems, their capacity for recovery and continued growth remains strong. Savings rates are high, government finances are stable, and the region has invested heavily in social and economic infrastructure. While the economic aspects of the 'miracle' may have been over-stated, East Asia has not been transformed overnight into a 'basket-case'. The causes of the present crisis vary, although some elements are shared across countries. Three factors have been of particular importance.

First, global demand for East Asian exports has slowed, diminishing the capacity of exports to sustain growth. In a region where exports have acted as the main engine of growth the consequences have been inevitably severe. Second, the US dollar has appreciated significantly against the yen, undermining the competitiveness of East Asian countries since most have tied their currency to the dollar. Countries with the least flexible exchange-rate regimes — notably Thailand — have faced the most acute adjustment pressures, losing market share to low-cost competitors such as China. Third, a combination of heavy foreign investment and weak financial regulation has allowed lenders to rapidly expand credit to high-risk borrowers, making financial systems increasingly vulnerable. In Thailand and Indonesia, banks and other financial institutions took out large, short-term dollar-denominated loans from foreign lenders, lending on to create a boom in real estate, and fuelling stock-market speculation. In South Korea, inadequate regulation of capital markets has enabled the giant *chaebol*, the conglomerates which dominate economic life, to borrow recklessly, destabilising the country's banking system in the process.

Foreign speculation and integration in global financial markets has increased the costs associated with financial mismanagement. But to blame ruthless foreign speculators for the currency crisis, as the Malaysian government has done, is dangerously misleading.[6] As we argue in this book, greater regulation of global markets is urgently needed in the interests of sustained growth, employment, and poverty reduction. However, improved regulation and sensible policy reforms are also needed at the national level. Serious policy mistakes have been made, which must not be repeated — and painful reforms must be pursued. Deeply corrupt political structures built on the foundations of 'crony capitalism', and family-run states, are not well-equipped to deal with the economic problems now facing East Asia. From South Korea's *chaebol* to the Suharto family empire in Indonesia, inefficient commercial enterprises have been granted privileged access to credit and state subsidies. The same motley collection of big business elites are now using their political influence to escape the costs of the crisis they have helped to cause.

Much will now depend on whether economic reform is backed by political reform. In some cases, the economic crisis is fuelling political transformation. In Thailand, the crisis has brought down a government and eased the passage of a new constitution. Similarly, in South Korea, a new government has been elected on a platform of cleaning up the financial corruption which contributed to the crisis in the banking system. In both cases, there have been moves towards improved financial transparency and accountability. Unfortunately, the same cannot be said of Indonesia and Malaysia. Whatever its past achievements and failings, the regime of President Suharto is now seen as a major part of Indonesia's problems. Pressure from the IMF has resulted in some limits being placed on favours for the Presidential family. But economic reforms are being grafted on to a political structure which functions on the basis of patronage and the use of public office to advance private gains, notably through subsidies, the granting of monopolies, and tariff protection. In Malaysia, populist bluster aimed in the general direction of the IMF and the industrialised countries has provided a smokescreen for domestic policy failure. The Petronas Tower in Kuala Lumpur was designed as the world's tallest building — and as a testament to Malaysia's economic strength. Instead, it has become a symbol of the ruinous property boom which, driven by irresponsible lending, has swept East Asia, diverting investment away from productive enterprise into speculative activity. The problem in Malaysia, as in Indonesia, is that the government is so firmly a part of the corrupt economic and financial structures behind the crisis that it cannot institute fundamental reforms without undermining its own positions.

Not all of the threats to East Asia's past achievements are domestic. Perhaps the greatest threat to continued growth and poverty reduction is located in Washington, at the headquarters of the IMF. For practical purposes, the IMF has assumed responsibility for formulating economic policy in countries with over 300 million citizens. It has done so without scrutiny, transparency or public accountability.[7] In these respects, it mirrors the problems associated with the governments with which it is now negotiating. The more serious problem is that the conditions associated with the IMF's 'rescue' operations now threaten to roll back the gains of the past. Just as it did in response to the Latin American debt crisis in the early 1980s, the Fund has responded to the East Asian crisis by demanding massive deflation, with cuts in public spending and high interest-rates as the main policy instruments.[8] This approach is not justified by the underlying economic conditions in East Asia where, in contrast to the position in Latin America in the 1980s, savings rates are high, inflation is low, and budgets are broadly in balance. Whatever the region's problems, East Asia is hardly a basket-case of fiscal profligacy. The danger now is that excessive deflation will turn recession into a full-blown depression, with its attendant consequences in terms of mass unemployment and rising poverty. There are already ominous parallels with Latin America, notably in the way that foreign-exchange shortages are undermining the capacity of potentially competitive companies to access imported technology.

Even less justified than the scale of deflation being imposed is the failure of the IMF (and the governments which have contributed to its operations) to consider the implications of its 'rescue' operations for the poor in the region. Perhaps several decades of rapid economic growth and poverty reduction have obscured the depth and severity of the poverty which remains. In Indonesia, deflation is being imposed on a country facing its worst drought in 50 years. This is a country in which one in ten of the population — over 20 million people — live in poverty. Millions more live perilously close to the poverty line, highly vulnerable to adverse economic trends. Moreover, extreme regional inequalities have left a huge poverty gap between Jakarta and some of the Outer Islands. In East Nussa Tengarra and West Kalimantan, where Oxfam works with local communities, poverty levels are in excess of 40 per cent. Field staff reports already indicate disturbing increases in poverty, as desperately poor rural households lose remittances from relatives in urban areas who are victims of the increase in unemployment. These are the words of one women, Rose Suares, a mother of six children living in Flores, in the Nusa Tengarra Timor Province of Indonesia: 'Without the earnings of my husband in Jakarta, I don't know how we will survive. How will I buy food, let alone find the fees for my children's school?' Her husband was among the first wave of 150,000 construction workers to lose their jobs. But her story is likely to become an increasingly common one, with an estimated one in five households in the Outer Islands depending on remittances from the 3 million migrant workers in Jakarta.

It is a similar story in Thailand, where unemployment is expected to increase by around 1 million over the next year. This has potentially devastating consequences for rural poverty in the north-east of the country, where over half of the absolute poor live, and where remittance levels are among the main determinants of welfare. While absolute poverty levels in Thailand are minimal, using the $1- a- day threshold, there are some 6 million Thais who live perilously close to that threshold, on incomes of $1 to $2 per day. Like Indonesia, Thailand will be required to undertake substantial cuts in public spending. This poses an immediate threat to the poor, who face a loss of basic social services in health and education. It also poses long-term threats to poverty reduction. East Asia's success has been built on the foundations of investment in human capital, which has created opportunities for health and education. These in turn have fuelled the process of economic growth. It follows that any erosion of the region's capital base will pose a threat to future growth.

None of this is inevitable. Less deflationary options designed to protect employment and public provision are available. Indeed, the danger is that excessive deflation will send regional economies into a nose-dive of declining investment and slow growth, undermining prospects for poverty reduction. Similarly, policy options are available which could restore stability without painful cuts in priority social services. What is needed at the outset is a political recognition of the potential threat to growth, equity, and poverty reduction posed by the current crisis, with the World Bank undertaking a review of the implications for the poor of its 'rescue' plans.

Looking to the future, there is another problem at the heart of the IMF's operation in East Asia: namely, the presumption in favour of creditors. Foreign creditor claims on the financial institutions of the region have been uncritically accepted as legitimate. This is despite the fact that reckless lending by Wall Street and European money markets is as much a feature of the crisis as domestic policy failure. As a *Financial Times* editorial has put it, the role of the IMF 'is not to bail out every idiot who has lent short-term to fund long-term investment'.[9] Unfortunately, this appears to be precisely what the management of the Fund regard as the institution's proper role.

But questionable as the IMF's adherence to deflationary economic policies may be, and as unacceptable as its domination by US and wider creditor interests undoubtedly is, there are positive elements in the conditions attached to the rescue packages. For instance, in Indonesia the IMF has demanded that President Suharto withdraws all tax and tariff exemptions, as well as subsidised loans, to the national car company owned by his son, Hutomo Mandala Poutra. The same son will lose his monopoly on the purchase of cloves, resulting in benefits for farmers. Major development projects, which would have transferred a large share of the budget to the Presidential family and associated cronies, have been abandoned or postponed. In South Korea, Indonesia, and Thailand, the IMF's loan conditions demand more effective surveillance of banks, and greater independence for central banks. All of this is long overdue. Ultimately, the precondition for successful constitutional reform is radical political change — and it remains to be seen whether or not the region's political systems can adapt.

The need for reform

Protecting the gains of the past and building upon them for the future poses enormous challenges to policy makers in East Asia. How can rapid economic growth be combined with sustainable resource management? What policies are needed to ensure an equitable sharing of national wealth? Can East Asia's autocratic political structures be reformed without conflict and instability? There are no easy answers. Major economic reforms are clearly needed. So too are institutional reforms. There is mounting evidence that economic growth is running up against the barriers presented by political autocracy. The region's institutions are debased and corrupted by their subordination to the pursuit of sectional self-interest. Their renewal demands the transition to more open and accountable political structures and a more constructive response to the calls for democracy now being heard across the region.

Flawed generalisations

Generalisations about the underlying causes of East Asia's 'success' are fraught with problems. The diversity of the region's countries and peoples, their historical differences, and differences in social and economic policy suggest the need for caution. Nonetheless, generalisations abound. Three schools of thought dominate efforts to explain East Asia's success. The first argues that authoritarian governance has been the central factor, with human rights being sacrificed on the altar of economic growth. One variant of this view is that universal human rights, as provided for in the UN Charter, are 'individualist', and therefore inconsistent with 'Asian values', which place the good of society above individual rights. The Malaysian Prime Minister has recently gone so far as to propose that the UN abandon its commitment to universal rights in order to accommodate East Asia, claiming that continued economic and social progress requires the suppression of individual liberties.[10] The second school of thought identifies free-market economic prescriptions as the critical factor in East Asia's success. In this account, trade liberalisation, financial deregulation, and adherence to market principles have acted as a springboard to efficiency, growth, and poverty reduction.[11] The World Bank has used East Asia's experience — or, more accurately, its own interpretation of that experience — to draw up a checklist of good policies, to be copied elsewhere. The third interpretation is essentially the reverse of the second. This stresses the central role of state intervention, protectionism, and financial regulation in driving East Asian growth.[12]

Each of these arguments suffers from a selective and inadequate interpretation of the evidence. Political factors are important in explaining poverty reduction in East Asia. But if authoritarianism were closely correlated with economic development, much of Africa and Latin America would be booming. Moreover, while political autocracy in East Asia delivered high growth in the past, it has also delivered the financial crisis and deep recession now gripping the region. The argument that democratic and accountable government is unable to develop long-term strategies for managing growth looks increasingly threadbare. Today, it is the inability of corrupt, unaccountable autocrats to disentangle economic policy from a complex web of corruption and private favours at the expense of the public purse, rather than the presumed short-comings of democracy, which poses the greatest threat to future prosperity. In short, the implied 'trade-off' between political freedom and progress towards poverty reduction is a myth. In reality, the notion of 'Asian values' is a euphemism for the violation of human rights on the part of political autocrats pursuing vested political and economic interests. In Malaysia, Indonesia, and Thailand exponents of East Asian 'values' receive funds from private interests, who claim repayments in the form of access to public funds and political favours provided at the expense of the poor. Leaving aside the wide variety of value systems in Asia, political protests in Indonesia, Thailand, and South Korea serve as a timely reminder that East Asian people, as distinct from their rulers, aspire to democracy and accountable government.

This book rejects the view that the economic success of East Asia is related to the preference of regional elites for autocracy and their predisposition to human rights violations. These are sources of weakness which threaten economic performance and future progress towards poverty reduction, rather than a source of strength. Nor is the secret of success to be found in adherence to free-market ideology. Markets have been important, but many of the policies advanced by the World Bank and others under structural adjustment run counter to those which have spurred poverty reduction and growth in East Asia. Governments across the region have adopted a wide variety of policies for regulating trade and investment, none of which conform to the free-market model favoured by international financial institutions such as the World Bank and the IMF. Moreover, Latin America and sub-Saharan Africa have embraced economic reforms with a conspicuous lack of success in terms of either growth or poverty reduction.[13] This is not to suggest, as do some critics of the World Bank-IMF view, that East Asia is a model of state-led growth through import substitution. Many of the mistakes associated with that model in sub-Saharan Africa, South Asia, and Latin America have been avoided in East Asia. Subsidies have been directed at specific industries in an effort to increase productivity and enhance competitiveness, but large and sustained budget deficits have been avoided. Similarly, protectionist measures have been used to provide domestic industries with the space to take root and develop; but currency overvaluation — and its corollary of unsustainable trade deficits — has been (until recently) conspicuous by its absence. Another important difference is that the specific forms of intervention adopted in East Asia have promoted labour-intensive (as opposed to capital-intensive) growth and enhanced productivity among smallholder producers. At the same time, strong and mutually reinforcing linkages have been established between growth and poverty reduction, with the expansion of opportunities for poor producers.

In this book we argue that East Asia's success in reducing poverty has been rooted in policies which combine growth and equity. Public investment in education and health, and the redistribution of productive assets, enabled the poor to produce their way out of poverty, contributing to economic growth in the process. Rather than facilitating the 'trickle down' of wealth through income redistribution, the East Asian model used the potential of the poor to act as agents of poverty reduction.

Structure of the book

This book examines the preconditions for growth with equity, and poverty reduction, drawing upon the experience of East Asia. Chapter 1 examines the broad background to East Asia's performance. It identifies policies for expanding health and education services, labour-intensive growth, and rural development as the central policies for combining growth with equity. Chapter 2 explains why growth and equity are important for poverty reduction. It points out that high levels of equity in the distribution of opportunities for production resulted in growth being more effective in reducing poverty in East Asia than in other developing regions; and that high growth has been an outcome, as well as a cause, of progress towards equity and poverty reduction. The claim that there is a trade-off between growth and equity, with gains in one area being possible only at the expense of costs in the other, is challenged.

Chapter 3 outlines the central role of social policy in creating the human development foundations for high growth and poverty reduction, contrasting the efficiency of social spending in East Asia with other developing regions. Five policy recommendations based on East Asia's experience are offered. In Chapter 4, we turn to policies for labour-intensive growth in manufacturing, which include selective protection and the regulation of foreign investment. Chapter 5 examines the importance of asset distribution to achieving growth with equity in rural development policies. It argues that, with supportive policies, small-holder production is inherently more efficient than large-scale agriculture, both as a vehicle for raising output and as a means of reducing poverty. There have been limits to growth with equity in East Asia, and these are examined in Chapter 6, with a focus on problems faced by Oxfam partners as a result of displacement, unregulated investment, and social marginalisation.

Finally, in Chapter 7, the origin of the current economic crisis affecting East Asia is examined, and the response of the international financial institutions critically assessed. There is an urgent need for concerted international action to protect the poorest and most vulnerable in the region, and recommendations for such action are outlined.

1 Three East Asian lessons

Interest in the East Asian 'model' has intensified since the World Bank claimed that the region's record was a testament to the success of free-market policies of the type associated with its structural adjustment programmes.[14] In fact, the East Asian 'model' is an invention designed to sustain a myth. There is no single model because the countries of the region have followed a diverse range of policies, reflecting their particular historical, political, and economic circumstances. With varying degrees of success, most have combined growth with equity and poverty reduction. But different countries have followed different routes — and they offer different lessons. The myth based on the East Asian 'model' is that governments in the region have adhered to free-market prescriptions. To the extent that there is any shared feature of economic policy it is to be found in a shared *rejection* of ideologically-driven free-market models of the type endorsed by the World Bank and the IMF. Indeed, many of the policies associated with structural adjustment are inconsistent with the policies which achieved rapid growth and poverty reduction in East Asia.[15]

Attempts to discover a single blue-print, designed in East Asia, which will be universally applicable are doomed to failure. That does not mean there are no lessons to be learned. Latin America and sub-Saharan Africa cannot blindly follow an East Asian path. Differences in the administrative capacity and political composition of states, differences in history and in economic wealth, will inevitably determine what is possible in particular regions and countries. But Taiwan did not follow South Korea, Indonesia did not follow Taiwan, and China and Vietnam have not followed Malaysia. Each country has developed specific policies conditioned by local circumstances. There are insights from each country: but they are different insights, and they vary over time. However, three broad lessons emerge from the range of national experience in East Asia: they are that poverty is not inevitable; that growth with equity is the key to poverty reduction; and that success in poverty reduction depends on political commitment.

Lesson 1
Poverty is not inevitable: a message for 2000

The first lesson is the most important — and the simplest. It is that rapid progress towards poverty eradication is possible. Four decades ago, anybody predicting the social and economic advances which have been achieved in East Asia would have risked public ridicule. Then, average incomes in South Korea were lower than in Zaire or Sudan. In the early 1970s, the incidence of poverty in Indonesia and Malaysia was comparable to that in much of sub-Saharan Africa and South Asia — and both countries were heavily dependent on exports of primary commodities. A Nobel Prize-winning economist confidently predicted a bleak future of economic stagnation and rising poverty. Indonesia was a prime 'basket-case' in the mid-1960s, burdened by an unsustainable debt, heavily dependent on aid, suffering from hyper-inflation, and chronically reliant on imported food.[16] The parallels with sub-Saharan Africa today are striking. In 1968, the author of one of the most influential books on development economics concluded that Indonesia 'must surely be accounted the number one failure among the major underdeveloped countries'.[17] He, too, predicted a future of slow growth and poverty.

Subsequent events in Indonesia and beyond provide a powerful lesson that nothing in human affairs — including poverty — is inevitable. As we show in Chapter 3, progress towards poverty reduction and economic growth has been sustained at rates which are without historical precedent. The achievements of East Asia since 1960 merit serious reflection on the part of the international community. Around the world today, an estimated 1.3 billion people — one-third of the developing world's population — live in poverty.[18] Malnutrition afflicts half a billion people, contributing to the loss through infectious disease of 25,000 child lives *every day*. Over 110 million children are denied the right to a basic education. As we approach the first decade of the twenty-first century, ending the human suffering associated with these cold facts is a moral imperative. Poverty should not be tolerated: what East Asia demonstrates is that the eradication of poverty is a practical possibility, and that poverty need not be tolerated.

This first lesson is an important one for the international community. At the World Summit for Social Development in 1995, governments committed themselves to 'the goal of eradicating poverty in the world through decisive national actions and international co-operation, as an ethical, social, political, and economic imperative of humankind'.

Ambitious targets were set for reducing child and maternal mortality, increasing literacy, and reducing malnutrition. The Programme of Action[19] adopted at the summit pledged by the year 2015 to:

- reduce the incidence of extreme poverty by 50 per cent;
- reduce infant and child mortality rates by two-thirds from their 1990 levels;
- reduce by three-quarters maternal mortality rates;
- achieve universal primary education in all countries.

Targets such as these are important because they establish yardsticks for measuring progress. But global averages are not enough. Progress must be achieved on a country-by-country basis, with governments in all countries judged against their performance. Two factors will dictate the prospects for success. First, accelerated economic growth will be required for a group of more than 130 developing countries. Second, increased investment in human development is both a requirement for accelerated growth, and a precondition for converting growth into poverty reduction. On both counts, East Asia provides insights into the policies needed to convert poverty reduction pledges from idle rhetoric into meaningful action.

Lesson 2 Growth with equity: the key to success

The second broad lesson to emerge from East Asia is that growth with equity holds the key to poverty reduction. For too long, debates about the relationship between growth and poverty have been characterised by an air of unreality. On the one side there are those who are mesmer - ised by economic growth, regarding it as the ultimate instrument for poverty reduction. On the other there are those who claim that growth leads only to continued poverty and widening inequalities. Both are slightly right — and both are badly wrong. Economic growth is vital to poverty reduction, but growth *can* result in some people becoming worse-off. Poor communities can be the victims of growth, for instance where they are displaced from their land by commercial investors, or by large-scale infrastructure projects. They can also be bypassed by growth, especially where they live in geographically remote areas. More broadly, wealthier people and regions tend to benefit more from economic growth than do their poorer counterparts, with the result that inequalities widen. But increasing inequality does not necessarily imply increased poverty. Contrary to the claims of growth pessimists, relatively few examples can be found of sustained growth in per capita income being associated with rising levels of poverty. However, growth optimists have turned a blind eye to the fact that widening inequalities can not only diminish the potential for translating growth into poverty reduction, but can also, as we suggest below, have the effect of slowing economic growth.

In short, economic growth, though essential for poverty reduction, is not enough. More research is needed to develop an understanding of how to optimise the poverty-reducing potential of growth. The World Bank has been at pains in recent years to refute the 'immisering growth' thesis (the notion that growth marginalises the poor or tends to impoverish significant sections of the population). An impressive body of evidence has been compiled to show that the incomes of the poor are increased by growth, and that a rising tide of wealth raises all boats. Unfortunately, much of this evidence is directed to demolishing the straw man erected by growth pessimists. What is needed is a better understanding of which patterns of growth bring most benefits to the poor. Why, for example, was China so much more successful in reducing poverty in the first half of the 1980s than in the second half, despite a strong growth performance in both periods? Why have levels of poverty in India fluctuated around a consistently modest downward trend which appears to be only weakly linked to growth performance? Why has Latin America's record on poverty reduction in the 1990s been so poor despite economic recovery? This book attempts to address some of these questions.

One of our conclusions is that the way in which wealth is created is as important as the volume of growth. The potential of growth to reduce poverty is optimised when the poor themselves act as agents of growth through their own production.[20] This has important policy implications. Income redistribution can play a central role in enhancing human development. More important, however, is the redistribution of the productive assets needed for wealth creation. These can take the form of tangible assets, such as land, credit, and water rights. Intangible assets, such as education and health, are equally vital to wealth creation, not least because of their implications for the productivity of tangible assets. It follows that effective poverty reduction strategies require redistribution in two areas: redistribution of tangible productive assets, and redistribution of human capital through pro-poor public spending.

Such strategies can enable poor people to participate in the growth process through the creation of opportunities. Markets are relatively efficient at allocating resources. But people enter markets with different endowments, in terms of the skills and assets they bring, and they receive different rewards. Changing the pattern of rewards in a pro-poor direction requires prior action to change the distribution of assets and human capital endowments (such as health and education). The linkages between growth and other aspects of human welfare, such as health, literacy, and life-expectancy, are far from automatic. Where most of East Asia scored far more highly than other developing regions has been in converting growth into poverty reduction and human development. This is precisely because economic growth has been combined with a high degree of equity in the distribution of income and, more importantly, access to opportunities for production, and to health and education services. In other words, greater equity in the distribution of rewards from the market has been based on the redistribution of assets and endowments in favour of the poor.

There is another reason for the positive interaction between growth and equity in East Asia. Widespread poverty, as well as being degrading in human terms and morally unacceptable, is also grossly inefficient in purely economic terms. Poverty reduces productivity, lowers the capacity for savings and investment, and restricts the development of dynamic markets.[21] The cycle is mutually reinforcing in a negative direction: lower productivity reduces incomes and future investment, which in turn reduces future output, income, and investment flows. Reduced purchasing power limits market opportunities for other producers, acting as a disincentive for production and employment creation. Poverty and inequity create negative linkages which are the mirror image of the positive linkages created by growth and equity.

The mechanisms for achieving growth with equity have been diverse. However, an important condition has been the creation of 'virtuous circles' of growth and human development. Growth in East Asia has self-evidently been good for poverty reduction. But policies for poverty reduction have also been good for growth, creating the conditions for rising productivity and output. One of the reasons why countries such as India, Brazil, and Mexico have failed to sustain growth, or to convert growth into poverty reduction, is that they have failed to make the necessary investments in human development. Where growth has occurred, it has trickled down to the poor at an abysmally slow pace. Meanwhile, the poor in East Asia have benefited from growth not because the gains have 'trickled down' to them, but because the development of their productive potential has been central to the growth process. Three interlocking policy elements have been crucial to the attainment of growth with equity and rapid poverty reduction: pre-poor social policies, redistributive rural development, and labour-intensive production.

Getting the social policy 'fundamentals' right

Much has been written about East Asia's economic success. Less widely appreciated is the fact that this success was built upon social foundations prepared before the surge in economic growth began. Improved levels of literacy and advances in public health-care enabled poor people to participate in economic growth, and to share more equitably in its benefits. It also enabled them to contribute to growth through improved productivity and adaptability. In most countries, social policy and economic policy operate on different tracks: the former concerned with welfare safety nets and the latter with growth. In East Asia, investment in human capital has been an integral part of growth-orientated economic policy. The focus has been not just on the provision of services, but on enhancing the access of poor people to these services.

Rural development through redistribution

With significant exceptions, East Asian countries have high levels of equity in the distribution of income and assets. Access to land, credit, and marketing infrastructure enabled the rural poor to produce and invest their way out of poverty. In turn, redistributive reforms in these areas helped to unleash the productive potential of the poor, reinforcing the linkages between high growth and a widespread sharing of its benefits. Dynamic smallholder agriculture, rather than large-scale commercial agriculture, has been one of the foundations for growth in East Asia.

Coherent policies for labour-intensive manufacturing

In contrast to most developing regions, economic growth in East Asia has been associated with high rates of employment creation. To varying degrees and at different times in different countries, market-oriented approaches to efficiency have been important. But a characteristic of these approaches has been their long-term time-frame. Selective protection, the regulation of foreign investment, and active industrial policy were all geared towards employment creation and improved productivity, which increased real wages. Elsewhere, especially in Latin America and Africa, protection and investment controls have been designed to promote capital-intensive growth with scant regard for efficiency, often penalising the poor in the process. The result has been slow growth and even slower rates of employment creation. Thus, countries such as Brazil, Mexico, and India have industrialised without significantly reducing poverty because they distorted interest rates, prices, and exchange rates to favour capital-intensive, rather than labour-intensive, industry.

Success in achieving growth with equity depends upon the successful integration of these three elements into a coherent policy framework. They cannot be selected on a pick-and-choose basis. Macro-economic reforms aimed at promoting employment and growth are unlikely to realise their potential without prior investment in human capital. China and Vietnam have sustained high rates of growth since the economic reforms of the late 1970s and mid-1980s respectively. But the human capital investment on which this growth was based was made two decades earlier. In India, by contrast, low levels of literacy and poor public health provision, the consequences of grossly inadequate social policy, have prevented the economic reforms introduced in 1991 from having any significant effects on growth and poverty reduction. Similarly, countries such as Mexico and Brazil may have liberalised their economies, but the inequitable distribution of productive assets has resulted in slow growth, and in the exclusion of the poor from its benefits. To some extent, good social policies can compensate for the effects of inequity in asset distribution, but only partially so. In Zimbabwe, public investment in health and education has contributed to impressive gains in human welfare. However, inequitable patterns of land ownership have contributed to high levels of poverty and slow growth, which has in turn reduced the resources available for social investment. What Zimbabwe has discovered in the 1990s is that good social policies need economic growth to sustain them, just as sustained growth requires good social policies.

Lesson 3 Political commitment

Political commitment is another pre-condition for achieving the successful integration of social and economic measures for poverty reduction. Pro-poor changes in policy direction in East Asia have often been a response to political crises. In Malaysia, the New Economic Policy was a response to the ethnic riots of the late 1960s.[22] Poverty and the marginalisation of the Malay community was perceived as a threat to national security, and poverty eradication through growth with equity was made a core element of economic policy. In Thailand, as in Malaysia, the sustained assault on poverty in the 1980s was a response to a growing awareness among the political elite of the threat to stability posed by poverty, especially in the north-east of the country. Earlier, in the 1950s and the 1960s, South Korea and Taiwan embarked on radical land reform and public investment, in part to head off similar threats posed by poverty. While the region's elites may be unaccountable, they have displayed a keen instinct for political survival, recognising the potential threat to their power inherent in high levels of poverty and social inequality. The major exception is the Philippines, which has suffered low growth and a high level of political instability as a consequence.

Here, too, there are lessons for the international community. Too often the response to global poverty has been to invest in containment, rather than in the creation of opportunity. The European Union responds to the refugee flows, health problems, and instability caused by conflict and social disintegration in Africa by investing in humanitarian aid for emergencies, and tightening migration controls, instead of directing its development co-operation efforts to addressing the social marginalisation and poverty which underlie the emergencies. The US responds to poverty in Latin America by tightening its border controls and attacking smallholders driven to produce drugs by the lack of alternative opportunities. This is the politics of responding to symptoms rather than dealing with causes. East Asia demonstrates the success of the opposite approach.

2 Growth with equity and poverty reduction

The facts of poverty reduction in East Asia speak for themselves.[23] In the mid-1970s, six out of every ten East Asians lived in poverty. Today, poverty affects roughly two out of every ten people. However, the absolute number of poor is still of staggering dimensions because of the size of the region's population. Around 345 million people were below the poverty line in 1995, which is more than in Latin America and sub-Saharan Africa combined. Even so, the progress towards poverty eradication has been spectacular. Over the period from 1975 to 1995 about 371 million people moved out of poverty, while the population increased by 425 million. (See Figure 1.) As a consequence, East Asia's share of world poverty declined to around 34 per cent, compared to 38 per cent a decade ago. The contrast with other developing regions is striking. In both South Asia and sub-Saharan Africa about half the population live in absolute poverty, as do one in four Latin Americans. Had sub-Saharan Africa matched East Asia's rate of poverty reduction, 100 million fewer of its people would be living in poverty.

Regional pictures obscure important variations between countries in East Asia. The Philippines has performed disastrously in terms of poverty reduction, with its share of the region's poor doubling to over 5 per cent since 1975. Progress towards income poverty reduction has also been slow in Vietnam, where over half of the population were poor in 1992, and in Lao PDR. Not only is poverty pervasive in both countries, with around one-half of their populations affected, but the depth of poverty (or the gap between the average income of those above and below the poverty line) is far wider than for other countries. By contrast, the two most populous countries in East Asia, China and Indonesia, have made the most dramatic advances, accounting for the bulk of the reduction in world poverty. In absolute terms, the number of poor has been more than halved in China and fallen by three-quarters in Indonesia. Translated into numbers, between 1970 and 1990:

- In China, 175 million people moved out of poverty, while the population increased by 300 million.

- In Indonesia, over 40 million people moved out of poverty, while its population increased by 60 million.

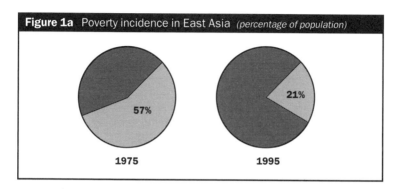

Figure 1a Poverty incidence in East Asia *(percentage of population)*

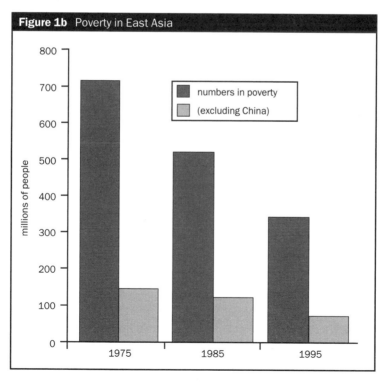

Figure 1b Poverty in East Asia

29

Indonesia's record in reducing the incidence of poverty from a starting point of low average incomes is particularly remarkable, with the percentage of poor falling from over 60 per cent to 11 per cent over the two decades to 1995. Impressive as this is, the proportional reductions were even greater in Malaysia (from 17 per cent to less than 1 per cent) and Thailand (from 8 per cent to less than 1 per cent). These achievements mark a continuation of past trends. By 1970, the first generation of 'tiger' economies — the 'newly industrialising countries' (NICs) of North-East Asia such as South Korea and Taiwan — had already made rapid strides towards poverty reduction.

The high levels of economic development achieved by these countries has tended to obscure the fact that all countries in the region have achieved high growth and poverty reduction from a starting point at which poverty was pervasive. In the mid-1960s, Indonesia's per capita income was lower than that of India, Bangladesh, and Nigeria. By the late 1980s, average income in Indonesia was 50 per cent higher than in Nigeria, 30 per cent higher than in India, and 150 per cent higher than in Bangladesh.

Income poverty is only one measure of deprivation. While it is closely related to other forms of deprivation in areas such as health and education, the links are not automatic. Most countries in East Asia have succeeded in combining a steep decline in income poverty with rapid advances in other areas. In 1960, average life expectancy in Indonesia was 41 years — lower than in India, and about two years longer than in Nigeria and Bangladesh. Today, life expectancy is two years longer than in India, twelve years longer than in Nigeria, and seven years longer than in Bangladesh. In China and Malaysia average life expectancy increased by eight years in the three decades after 1970. Infant mortality rates for the region have fallen by almost half.

Economic growth and rising average incomes have contributed to these gains, in part by creating additional resources for social investment; and in part because rising average incomes are positively linked to improved nutritional status. According to some accounts, the social achievements of countries in the first generation of NICs, such as South Korea, can be traced to differences in economic strength. There is an element of truth in such accounts. For instance, disparities in social-sector spending capacity clearly affect human development outcomes. South Korea spends almost $400 per capita on health care, while Uganda spends around $3. Inevitably, the disparity in spending contributes to disparities in health outcomes. As we show in Chapter 4, however, the quantity of social-sector spending cannot fully account for the differences in outcomes between East Asia and the rest of the developing world.

Important as economic growth may be, many countries in the region achieve high levels of human development despite their low levels of average income. For instance (adjusted for purchasing power parity):

- In Vietnam, average per capita income is comparable to that in Nigeria, but average life expectancy is 15 years longer, children are twice as likely to reach their fifth birthday, and the literacy rate is twice as high.

- Indonesia has the same average income as Peru, but over 90 per cent of its citizens have access to health services. In Peru, the comparable figure is 56 per cent — and the health services in question are vastly inferior.

Vietnam provides proof positive that low income is not a barrier to progress in poverty reduction. Even with a per capita income of $200 — less than the average for sub-Saharan Africa — rapid advances in human welfare have been achieved. Since 1980, life expectancy has increased by four years, and the Infant Mortality Rate has fallen from 57 to 42 per 1000 live births. Adult literacy is over 90 per cent, and 93 per cent of the population has access to health services, compared to about 50 per cent in Africa. Along with most of East Asia, Vietnam has achieved these advances through social and economic policies which create opportunities for the poor. This is good news for governments with a commitment to poverty reduction in other countries. For instance, the Government of Uganda is developing an integrated strategy for poverty reduction, including early moves towards the achievement of universal primary education (see Chapter 3). With around 40 per cent of children of primary-school age out of school, the challenge is an enormous one. However, Vietnam, which has an average income only slightly higher than Uganda (adjusted for purchasing parity) but has achieved almost universal enrolment, shows that such efforts can succeed. Viewed in a different perspective, the achievements of Vietnam, China, and Indonesia are an indictment of the failure of governments, not only in the poor countries of sub-Saharan Africa and South Asia, but also in far wealthier countries such as Brazil and Mexico. Consider, for example, the comparison between China and Brazil in Figure 2. Average incomes in Brazil are more than five times higher than those in China. Despite this, the proportion of the population living below the poverty line is the same in both countries, while a Brazilian citizen faces a considerably higher risk of dying before the age of 40. The huge gulf in income inequality level between the two countries demonstrates the importance of distributional equity in influencing human welfare outcomes.

Striking inequalities in the distribution of income, land, and opportunity in Latin America have locked the region into the reverse of East Asia's virtuous circle of growth and human development. More equitable income distribution would have the effect of raising savings and investment levels, thereby fuelling economic growth. It would also help to expand school enrolment, which is one of the most decisive factors in the long-term growth process and a primary determinant of income inequality. Similarly, greater equity in the distribution of public investment in health and education would generate high returns for both growth and human development.

Differences in human development outcomes between East Asia and other regions underline the importance of combining equity with growth. Poor people in East Asia have gained a bigger share in the production and distribution of wealth; and they have gained from social policies which have delivered basic services. Quality has been variable and there have been significant gaps in coverage, but measured against the yard-stick of equity in public investment, efficiency has been high in comparison with other regions, with strong human welfare returns for each dollar invested. We examine some of the reasons for this in Chapter 3.

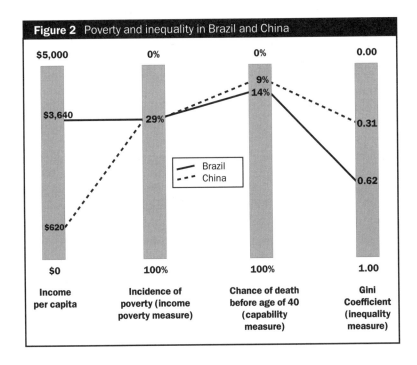

Figure 2 Poverty and inequality in Brazil and China

Accompanying East Asia's poverty reduction 'miracle' has been the more widely publicised 'economic miracle'. For almost four decades, countries in the region have sustained unprecedented rates of economic growth. The slow-down in economic growth in East Asia since 1996, and the recent currency crisis, have prompted a wave of obituary notices; it remains to be seen whether these reports of the death of East Asia's economic miracle are premature. However, the decline has to be set in context. Average GDP growth for East Asia in 1997 (excluding China) is projected at between 1 and 3 per cent,lower than for sub-Saharan Africa and Latin America. Looking back over a longer period of two decades, however, national incomes in East Asia have roughly doubled every six to eight years. Central to this achievement has been East Asia's success in penetrating world markets with increasingly sophisticated and higher-value-added products.

As Figure 3 shows, East Asia has separated from large swathes of the developing world by a yawning growth gap, which has been widening since the 1960s, and continued to widen in the 1990s. In the first half of the decade, average incomes in the region increased by over 8 per cent a year. In South Asia and Latin America, they have grown by around 2 per cent and 1 per cent respectively, on average. In sub-Saharan Africa, income

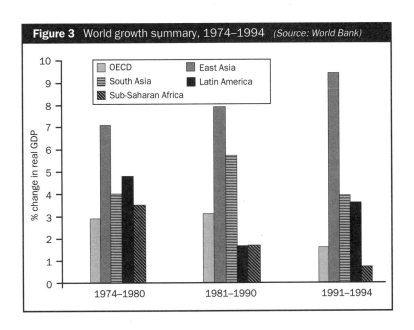

Figure 3 World growth summary, 1974–1994 *(Source: World Bank)*

levels have fallen. Only six out of 49 countries in the region (accounting for less than 5 per cent of its population) have achieved higher levels of income in the 1990s than they had in the past.[24] The resulting shift in relative incomes reflects Africa's growing marginalisation. In 1965, average per capita incomes in the region were 60 per cent of the developing country average; today they are 30 per cent. Nor is it only Africa which is suffering the consequences of marginalisation. Out of 167 countries reviewed by the United Nations Development Programme (UNDP) for the 1997 Human Development Report, 97 had lower incomes in 1996 than in 1990.[25]

Linking growth to poverty reduction

Differences in growth rates have had an important bearing on regional differences in poverty reduction and human development. Growth is important for poverty reduction because it determines the size of the economic cake: the goods and services which are available. In poor countries, increases in the supply of income-generating resources are a necessary condition for improving entitlements to economic goods through employment and production. Without growth, it is impossible to sustain improvements in human welfare and achieve rapid poverty reduction. However, economic growth *alone* is an insufficient condition for advancing human development. Equally important is the distribution of growth: how the economic cake is divided between different groups in society — for instance, between rich and poor, or between men and women — has a critical bearing on poverty reduction.

So, too, does another consideration: namely, who participates in the baking of the cake, and on what terms. Economists often reduce social welfare questions to considerations of growth and income distribution. But the distribution of productive assets is also critical. These assets include not only what is conventionally described as physical or financial capital (land, productive inputs, savings, and credit), but also human capital, for example, education and health. Both education and health are important as ends in themselves, because they enhance the quality of life and extend the range of choice for individuals. As such, they represent an important yardstick for measuring human development. However, they are equally important as means to the end of economic growth and equity. Higher levels of education and better health enable poor people to contribute more fully to the growth process, and to participate more equitably in the opportunities which growth creates and the benefits it offers.[26] In other words, the greater the degree of involvement in baking the cake, the better the prospect of receiving a bigger slice! Equity in this wider sense means more than the equitable distribution of income. It means the wider distribution of opportunities for participation in social and economic life, which is in turn influenced by the distribution of power at various levels: between rich and poor people, men and women, different regions, and ethnic groups, to name but four dimensions.

Growth has acted as a powerful driving force for poverty reduction in East Asia. The relationship between growth and poverty reduction is much debated — and the picture varies from country to country, as we show below. Without growth, however, it would not have been possible to achieve the social advances which have been made in East Asia. When China's economic reforms began in 1978, the country was a desperately poor rural economy. Over half of its citizens lived on less than the World Bank poverty line income of $1 a day. Since 1978, average incomes in China have expanded four-fold. To put this figure in context, Chinese incomes are currently doubling every ten years. In Britain it took almost 60 years for incomes to increase by a similar amount after the industrial revolution. The implications of high growth can be illustrated by a further comparison of China with the UK. Over time, even a small change in the rate of growth can deliver large increases in income, and transform the income position of households. Were China's 7 per cent growth rate to be sustained over the lifetime of an average Chinese citizen born today, their real income at the end of their lives would be 160 times what it was at birth. Over the same period, average incomes in China would rise from 14 per cent of those in the UK to 500 per cent. Of course, such projections need to be treated with caution; it is easier to catch up than overtake. Even so, the figures do point to some revolutionary implications for the global economy.[27]

Equally revolutionary has been the impact of growth on poverty and human welfare in China. Between 1978 and 1995, 200 million people were lifted out of poverty, over half of them living in rural areas.[28] Allied to the reduction of poverty has been a dramatic improvement in other development indicators, with life expectancy ten years longer today than in 1970.

There is a painful contrast between this experience and the typical pattern in other developing regions. Nowhere are the contrasts more painful than in South Asia. In Pakistan, economic growth has created the potential for achieving sustained human welfare advance, with per capita incomes rising by 230 per cent between 1970 and 1990.[29] Yet at the end of this period, Pakistan's human welfare indicators make miserable

35

reading. An additional 17 million people have fallen below the poverty line, and the incidence of poverty is now higher than it was in the mid-1980s.[30] Two-thirds of the country's adult population and three-quarters of women are illiterate. Basic health facilities are available to only half the population, and one-quarter of newborn children are underweight.[31] Such facts demonstrate the way in which inequalities rooted in national power structures and the debasement of political institutions can pre-empt the gains of economic development.

In terms of poverty reduction, the quality of growth has been as important as the quantity. East Asia has differed from other developing regions not only in its rate of growth, but in the extent of conversion of growth into poverty reduction. One way of capturing these differences is to compare the 'poverty elasticity' of growth rate, that is, the percentage decrease in the number of poor people associated with each percentage point of growth. In Malaysia, and Indonesia, every percentage point of growth reduces the number of poor people living below the poverty line by around 3 per cent, or more.[32] Recent World Bank research has shown a more variable picture for China, which is outlined below. However, the dramatic progress towards poverty reduction during the first half of the 1980s was achieved by a poverty elasticity of growth rate of around 3.6 per cent. For most of Africa, the poverty elasticity of growth rate is below 2 per cent, and only 1.4 per cent in Nigeria, the region's most populous country.[33] In Brazil, the most populous country in Latin America, each percentage point increase in economic growth produces a reduction in the number of poor people of less than 1 per cent.

These figures have an obvious practical relevance, in that countries with a low growth elasticity of poverty reduction have to grow faster than those with higher elasticities in order to achieve comparable results. Between 1990 and 1995, per capita economic growth in Latin America averaged slightly over 2 per cent per annum. Despite this, the number of poor and indigent people in the region rose from 197 million to 209 million, according to the Economic Commission for Latin America (ECLA).[34] The number of poor people has remained 50 million above the average for the 1980s, while the overall incidence of poverty fell by only 1 per cent, to 33 per cent, between 1990–1995. Even less success was achieved in the reduction of 'indigence', defined as the inability to meet basic food needs. This fell from 18 per cent to 17 per cent. As a result, one out of six households in Latin America would still not be in a position to satisfy basic nutritional needs, even if the entire household income was spent on food. Clearly, very little of the economic growth achieved during the 1990s in Latin America has trickled down to the poorest sections of society, and the numbers affected by poverty remain higher than in 1980. One reason for this poor performance is that, in all but one country (Uruguay), the richest 10 per cent have increased their share of national income, while the poorest 40 per cent have seen their shares stagnate or decline. Latin America illustrates in extreme form how inequity can act as a catalyst for poverty. During the 1980s, the Gini coefficient for the region rose by 4 points as the poorest 20 per cent saw their income shares shrink. Had this shift in income distribution not taken place, the number of additional people falling below the poverty line would have been cut by half. Expressed differently, half of the rise in income poverty — representing 50 million people — was due to a redistribution in favour of the rich. The failure to introduce redistributive policies has contributed to a slow-down in poverty reduction since 1994, with only three countries recording progress and four — Mexico, Argentina, Honduras, and Venezuela — suffering an increase in poverty levels. Without dramatic changes in the quality of growth in Latin America, there is no prospect of achieving income poverty reduction on the scale required. (See Figure 4 showing the incidence of poverty in Latin America.)

The same applies even more strongly to sub-Saharan Africa. Just under half of the region's population — around 219 million people — live below the income poverty line, rising to over 60 per cent in countries such as Zambia, Mozambique, and Burkina Faso. Numbers are increasing both in proportionate and absolute terms. According to highly optimistic World Bank projections, per capita incomes in the region will grow by 1.2 per cent for the next decade. Even if this target were reached, it would not be remotely adequate for reducing poverty on the scale required because of the weak linkage between growth and poverty reduction. At best, average incomes would be no higher in 2006 than in 1987, and 5 per cent lower than they were in 1974.[35] So the next decade offers at best only a partial recovery of ground lost in the 1980s. Assuming that current income distribution patterns remain intact, this would leave between one-quarter and one-third of the population below the poverty line during the middle years of the next century.

In South Asia, which is home to the greatest number of poor people, the linkage between growth and poverty reduction has been weak since the mid-1980s. Between 1987 and 1993 the incidence of income poverty (measured against a poverty line of $1 per day) remained virtually unchanged at around 43 per cent. In countries such as India and Pakistan, progress towards poverty reduction has been slow since the mid-1980s, while the absolute number of poor people has continued to rise. During the 1990s, economic growth in Pakistan has slowed, even though it has remained positive in per capita terms. However, a combination of inflation, rising taxes, and deep inequalities has increased the incidence of poverty from around 20 per cent to 30 per cent, adding around 18 million people to the ranks of the absolute poor.[36] In India, the linkages between growth and poverty reduction have been stronger. As economic growth accelerated between the mid-1970s and mid-1980s the proportion of the population in absolute poverty fell by 2.4 per cent per year — three times the rate in the previous decade. However, growth and poverty reduction linkages have not been strong enough to prevent an increase in the absolute number of people living in poverty. Thus, while the incidence of poverty has declined from one in two to one in three since 1951, the number of poor has grown from 164 million to 312 million.[37] The contrast with Indonesia is striking. Between 1970 and 1993, the proportion of Indonesia's population living in poverty fell by a factor of seven, from 58 per cent of the population to 8 per cent, or by 10 per cent a year.[38]

Income distribution and poverty reduction

Differences in the distribution of income are central to inter-regional differences in poverty reduction. One way of viewing these differences is to compare the shares of national income going to the richest and poorest sections of society. Figure 5 summarises data for 13 countries, for illustrative purposes. Assuming that income from growth is distributed on the basis of existing patterns, it is possible to derive some striking insights into why growth and poverty reduction are so weakly correlated in some countries, and so strongly correlated in others. In the case of Brazil, which ranks fifth in the world league table for numbers in

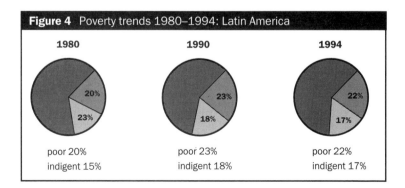

Figure 4 Poverty trends 1980–1994: Latin America

1980	1990	1994
20%	23%	22%
23%	18%	17%
poor 20%	poor 23%	poor 22%
indigent 15%	indigent 18%	indigent 17%

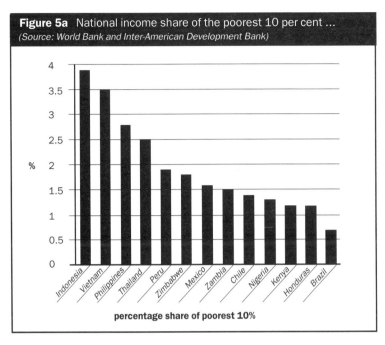

Figure 5a National income share of the poorest 10 per cent ...
(Source: World Bank and Inter-American Development Bank)

percentage share of poorest 10%

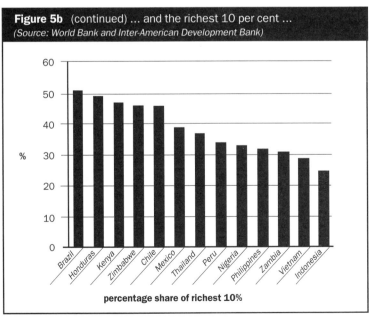

Figure 5b (continued) ... and the richest 10 per cent ...
(Source: World Bank and Inter-American Development Bank)

percentage share of richest 10%

absolute poverty, for every $1 generated in growth the poorest 10 per cent of the population receive less than 1 cent, while the wealthiest 10 per cent receive 50 cents — double the amount received by their counterparts in Indonesia and Vietnam. Such patterns explain why it takes a lot of growth to bring a few benefits to the poor in Brazil and elsewhere in Latin America.

There is a notable exception to the generally positive picture in East Asia: in the Philippines, the income share of the richest 20 per cent is 11 times that of the poorest, compared to five times in Indonesia. Skewed income distribution has contributed to the poor performance of the Philippines in reducing poverty. In the two decades to 1990, poverty fell by 1 per cent a year, which was less than half the rate achieved by Malaysia, Thailand and, from a weaker economic base, Indonesia.

Income distribution patterns make it clear that some countries would have to grow very fast to achieve even moderate progress. In order for the poorest 10 per cent of the population to receive the equivalent amount of income from growth:

- Mexico would have to grow at roughly four times the rate of South Korea;

- Brazil would have to grow at seven times the rate of Indonesia;

- Zimbabwe would have to grow at more than twice the rate of Vietnam;

- Kenya would have to grow at over twice the rate of Thailand.

A change in the pattern of income distribution can have important implications for poverty, for better or for worse. The better case is illustrated by Malaysia. Until 1970, economic growth in the country was relatively strong, averaging 6 per cent in the 1960s, but accompanied by widening income inequality, with the share in national income of the poorest 20 per cent declining.[39] Progress towards poverty reduction was slow, with about 60 per cent of the population estimated to be below the poverty line at the end of the 1960s. 'Trickle down' was not working for the poor. In 1971, the 'New Economic Policy' was adopted, giving a high priority to equity and poverty reduction.[40] Social programmes absorbed 60 per cent of budget spending, with a focus on smallholder producers and marginal areas. Growth increased, but not dramatically so; far more dramatic was the reduction in the incidence of poverty. Using national poverty lines, this fell from 60 per cent to around 18 per cent. While Malaysia has remained one of the most unequal East Asian countries, improved income distribution was central to this achievement, with the income share of the poorest 20 per cent rising by one-third between 1973 and 1987.[41]

The worse-case scenario is provided by Latin America. During the 1980s, average incomes in the region declined under the weight of economic collapse and the debt crisis. Income distribution also changed in favour of the wealthy, with the average income of the top 20 per cent rising from a multiple of ten times the income of the poorest 40 per cent to a multiple of 12.[42] Over the same period an additional 100 million people fell below the poverty line. According to the Inter-American Development Bank (IDB) half of this increase in poverty was a direct consequence of the change in the pattern of income distribution.[43] Such facts have an obvious bearing on the distribution of poverty. Average per capita income in Indonesia is half that of Peru, yet in Peru about 50 per cent of the population live in income poverty — three times the percentage in Indonesia. If the incidence of income poverty in Indonesia was the same as it is in Peru, another 830 million Indonesians would be poor.

Progress towards poverty reduction has not been uniform in East Asia. In China, the most rapid gains were made in the period 1978-1984, as the decollectivisation of agriculture and the associated increase in rural prices and output boosted rural incomes. Because of the concentration of poverty in rural areas, rapid growth in this period was accompanied by a move towards greater equality and poverty reduction. Over the next five years, rural productivity growth slowed, prices stagnated, and growth was concentrated in coastal areas. As a consequence, progress towards poverty reduction slowed and inequalities widened. This picture continued until 1992, after which rural incomes began to increase more strongly (dramatically so, with a rise in grain prices during 1994-1995).[44] Thus during the 1990s, progress towards poverty reduction has resumed, albeit in the context of widening inequalities. Important lessons can be derived from China's experience. Perhaps the most important is the need to look beyond broad growth aggregates, to the prices for goods produced and consumed by poor people, and the productivity and output trends in the sectors where poor people pursue their livelihoods. In the case of China, it was when GDP growth translated into growth in rural per capita incomes that the incomes of the poor increased most rapidly, pointing to the importance of development strategies which unlock the productive potential of the rural poor.

Growth and equity: the 'trade off' myth

Policies to redistribute productive assets, and public investment in favour of the poor, are obvious strategies for achieving more equitable patterns of income distribution. However, there is a widely held view that redistributive measures are self-defeating because they slow economic growth, thereby reducing the flow of resources needed to reduce poverty. There is, so this argument runs, a trade-off between equity on the one side and growth on the other. Another received wisdom of development economics is that high rates of growth and the structural changes associated with them (such as rapid urbanisation) inevitably cause increased inequality.[45] Many economists have further argued that inequality is good for growth, since it concentrates resources in the hands of sections of the population which are most likely to invest them, and hence contribute to capital accumulation and more rapid growth.[46] Do such arguments stand?

The evidence provided in Figure 6 suggests not. This clusters countries by measuring their performance in terms of economic growth against their income distribution patterns, as indicated by the Gini coefficient, a measure of how income distribution deviates from a hypothetical situation in which everybody has exactly the same income. Deviations from 0 (perfect equality) to 1 (total inequality) indicate the extent of inequality. Admittedly, the methodology provides at best a limited indicator of the causal relationships at play. The Gini coefficient provides only a static snapshot based on average figures, thereby obscuring the dynamic interaction between distribution and growth patterns. Also, distributional factors are only one among several factors, and their effects are not isolated in this snapshot. With these considerations in mind, what does the exercise tell us? At one level, not a great deal. The picture which emerges is inconclusive. Countries such as Botswana and Chile illustrate that it is perfectly possible to combine high growth with high levels of inequality, with obvious costs for poverty reduction. Two East Asian countries — Malaysia and Thailand — veer towards this group. Others — such as India — demonstrate that it is equally possible to combine relatively high levels of equality with low growth. Most, however, succeed in achieving the worst of all possible worlds: namely, high inequality together with low growth. Much of Africa and Latin America fits into this category, although East Asia is also represented, by the Philippines. With its Latin American-style structure of land ownership and income distribution, this country is a worst-case example. At the other end of the spectrum, in the north-west

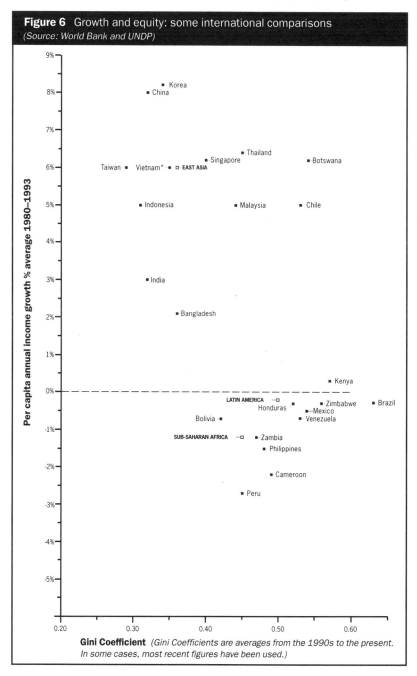

Figure 6 Growth and equity: some international comparisons
(Source: World Bank and UNDP)

corner of the scatter graph, lie the majority of East Asian countries, indicating their success in combining economic dynamism with equity.

The message which emerges is clear: a high degree of inequity tends to be bad not only for poverty reduction, but also for growth. Rather than being associated with higher growth, high levels of inequality appear to be a constraint on growth. In the case of Latin America, there is now a substantial body of research suggesting that higher levels of inequality help to explain the region's slower growth in comparison to East Asia. It follows that governments which are serious about growth should get serious about equity and redistribution. East Asia's experience demolishes the myth that there is a necessary trade-off between growth and equity, with gains in one area being achieved at the expense of the other. China is one of the world's fastest-growing economies and also one of its most equal. Moreover, not only have the East Asian countries remained relatively equal by international standards, several — including Korea and Malaysia — have achieved improved equity with growth. More recently, income inequalities in the region have been widening in most countries, though economic history suggests that this trend is neither inevitable nor desirable.

The linkages between income distribution and poverty reduction are relatively clear. So, too, are those between growth and poverty reduction. But how does inequality affect growth? And if the benefits of growth continue to reach the poor, does inequality matter? These questions need to be addressed at various levels. In economic terms, there are good reasons why inequality may constrain growth. Where income distribution is highly skewed it limits the savings and investment potential of the poor, with damaging implications for output and employment. Because the poor are credit constrained and precluded by virtue of their poverty from reducing consumption in order to finance investment, they are unable to make investments which could yield very high returns in terms of output.[47] By increasing the incomes of the poor, reducing inequality can help to create a virtuous circle of rising investment and increased returns to labour, culminating in higher savings and future investment.[48] High levels of inequality and poverty are also associated with other factors which obstruct growth. They limit the size of the market, hence acting as a disincentive and limiting the creation of economic linkages, notably between urban and rural sectors. Such factors explain why a number of comparative economic studies have found a close association between greater inequality and lower growth.[49] Income inequalities are a consequence as well as a cause of other forms of inequality, for instance in the distribution of productive assets, which can hamper growth. For instance, highly concentrated patterns of land ownership in Latin America tend to be associated with lower levels of efficiency and investment in agriculture.[50]

To the extent that effective poverty reduction depends on growth, patterns of inequality which lower growth will have adverse consequences for poverty. There is also a more dynamic interaction between distribution and poverty reduction: where poor people are excluded from opportunities by inadequate access to productive assets, and to health and education provision, their incomes are likely to be low, and society suffers from the loss of their productive potential. The result is sub-optimal growth and sub-optimal progress towards poverty reduction. It follows that social and economic progress can be retarded by rising inequalities in opportunity. Conversely, greater equity in the distribution of opportunites can have positive benefits for both growth and human development. The common denominator of shared growth policies in East Asia was that they relied on enhancing the productivity of the poor, rather than relying on welfare transfers to raise incomes. At the other end of the policy spectrum is Latin America, where there was no attempt to redistribute opportunities through land reform, or to invest in the health and education of the poor. Ironically, welfare transfers played a bigger role in Latin America than in East Asia, but were insufficient to counteract the negative effects on growth of high levels of inequality and poverty.

There are other, less immediately quantifiable and tangible, factors which link growth and distribution. Where the benefits of growth accrue to easily identifiable social groups and bypass other groups, social tensions can result. Imbalances between urban and rural populations, between different ethnic groups, and different regions, can become politically destabilising, even in a context of overall progress towards poverty reduction. This is apparent in East Asia, where the rapid accumulation of wealth has been accompanied by a growing perception that its distribution is unfair (see Chapter 6).

None of this is to deny that, for governments perverse enough to regard the option as desirable, it is possible to combine high growth with worsening trends in income equality. But, leaving aside whether this is morally acceptable, it is certainly questionable whether high growth can be sustained over the long term in the absence of progress towards human development and equity.

Chile illustrates the problems in extreme form. Despite an economic recovery starting in the second half of the 1970s and continuing (after a collapse in the early 1980s), the percentage of households living in poverty doubled between 1970 and 1990.[51] Income inequalities also widened, with the share of national income going to the richest 10 per cent increasing from 10 per cent to 37 per cent. The Gini coefficient increased from 0.45 to 0.57, one of the most dramatic increases in inequality of this period. Falling real wages, the reversal of previous land redistribution measures, and a stringent stabilisation programme were the main factors behind this trend. The rapid increase in growth achieved after 1984 is often cited as evidence that the trade-off between growth and equity, while painful, was necessary and unavoidable. In fact, the evidence can be interpreted differently. Economic growth did not accelerate until after 1986, coinciding with a move towards equity and poverty reduction. This trend has continued into the 1990s. In Chile, stronger growth has been accompanied by improvements in equity, while the initial deepening of inequality was accompanied by slow growth. Whatever the nature of the association between growth and equity, there can be little doubt that the depth of inequality in Chile has limited the potential for converting growth into poverty reduction.

Income differences, as measured by Gini coefficients in Figure 6, represent only one aspect of inequality. They are the outcome of other forms of inequality. The distribution of opportunities for employment, and of productive assets such as land and credit, and of access to health care and education, are more fundamental determinants of equity. They are also among the primary determinants of growth, helping to explain the picture summarised in Figure 3. Countries in Latin America, South Asia, and sub-Saharan Africa are slow growing, partly because of inequities in the distribution of opportunities. Establishing the precise impact of inequality on growth is problematic. However, recent research carried out for the OECD has attempted to quantify the effects by using eocnometric models. some of the most striking simulations emerge from comparisons of Brazil and Korea. These suggest that if, in 1960, Korea had Brazil's level of equality, its growth rate over the net 25 years would have been 0.6 per cent less each year, implying a 15 per cent reduction in average income.[52]

If countries in East Asia demonstrate the benefits of positive linkages between growth and equity, India demonstrates the costs of negative linkages. From the mid-1970s to the end of the 1980s, the country made progress towards poverty reduction. However, during the second half of the 1980s, the rate of rural poverty reduction slowed from 5 per cent to 1 per cent a year, even while the rate of overall economic growth increased.[53] The economic reform programme introduced in 1991 was intended to boost economic growth, by reducing protection and bureaucratic controls on industry, and to accelerate poverty reduction by creating new opportunities for the poor. It has done neither. After an initial spurt, economic growth rates for the 1990s have, on average, fallen below those achieved in the 1980s; while the incidence of poverty in rural areas has increased, and in urban areas has fallen only marginally.

Why has India failed to translate growth into poverty reduction? Partly because in rural areas, where three-quarters of the poor live, inadequate efforts have been made to distribute opportunities. Land and tenancy reforms have not been implemented in most states, weakening the capacity of poor people to take advantage of the opportunities offered by economic growth.

Growth and human development: China and India compared

The dynamic interaction between growth and human development is apparent from a comparison of China and India. In the 1950s, both countries had comparable human welfare indicators. Until the 1980s, they also had comparably slow growth rates. Where they diverged was in their human development performance. By the early 1980s China was ranked as the twenty-second poorest country in the world, but it ranked 23 places higher on the UNDP's Human Development Index because of its strong performance in improving human welfare.[54] Today, China is still a low-income country but it is ranked in the UNDP's medium human development category, 30 places above India. The differences with India are striking:

- Life expectancy in India today is 12 years shorter than in China — and five years shorter than it was in China three decades ago.

- Around half of India's population is illiterate (rising to 70 per cent for women in some states). In 1991, adult literacy rates for Indian women were 34 per cent. In China, female literacy stood at 85 per cent in 1980.

- Half of all Indian girls aged between 5 and 14 do not attend school. In China, the non-attendance rate is around 5-7 per cent.

- China's infant mortality rate is one-third that of India. In India, one-third of all newborn babies are underweight, reflecting the nutrition and health deprivation suffered by women, and one-half of children suffer chronic malnutrition — five times the incidence in China.

- Maternal mortality in India is over four times higher than in China (437 compared to 95 per 100,000). One in four of all women whose death is related to childbearing is Indian.

While almost one-half of India's population live in income poverty, about two-thirds are 'capability poor' — that is, they do not receive minimum levels of education and health care.[55] The human costs of India's human development deficit are self-evident. High levels of illiteracy and poor public health are consequences of the country's inadequate social welfare provision. That weakness has served to exclude the poor from growth, and to weaken the links between growth and poverty reduction. Despite a growth rate of around 5 per cent in the second half of the 1980s, poverty reduction began to slow down. The economic reforms of 1991 have not changed this picture. Rapid industrialisation in states such as Gujerat, the emergence of high technology industries in Bangalore, the growth of Bombay as a financial centre, and images of Bangalore's nascent car industry as Asia's Detroit-in-the-making, all obscure the deeper reality of a failure to achieve poverty reduction levels on anything like the scale required. According to the UNDP's 1997 *Human Development Report*, rural poverty levels in India today are similar to those in 1986.[56]

For the vast majority of the 320 million Indian citizens living in poverty, suffering poor health, and lacking basic reading and writing skills, economic reform has brought few benefits. One reason, as Jean Dreze and Armatya Sen have argued, is lack of education: 'The abysmal inequalities in India's education system represent a real barrier against widely sharing the fruits of economic progress...Even if India were to take over the bulk of the world's computer software industry, this would still leave its poor, illiterate masses largely untouched.'[57] India's massive deficit in human capital weakens the linkages between urban-based industrial growth and poverty reduction, especially in the rural areas where almost 80 per cent of the poor live. Low levels of educational achievement are among the most powerful structural forces weakening the conversion of growth into poverty reduction. Poor education is also among the strongest forces for transmitting poverty across generations: with 33 million children between six and ten years old not in school, the future potential for growth to reduce poverty is being diminished.[58] There is a vicious circle at work here, since many poor households are forced to withdraw children from school in order to raise household income and output. According to some estimates, there are over 100 million child workers in India.[59]

Differences between Indian states illustrate the strong relationships between education coverage and other indicators for human development and poverty reduction. For instance, Kerala has achieved the strongest educational performance of any Indian state, and health indicators which are far higher than the Indian average. The state has also effectively eliminated the extreme gender biases which characterise health and education in India. The upshot is the most impressive poverty-reduction outcomes, even in comparison to states where average incomes are far higher. Since the mid-1950s, Kerala has sustained an annual decline in rural poverty of around 2.4 per cent. This is 120 times higher than in Bihar, where the female literacy rate is 18 per cent, and four times more than Rajasthan, where the female literacy rate is 20 per cent. In Madhya Pradesh, where female life expectancy is 20 years lower, the annual poverty reduction rate is one-sixth of that achieved in Kerala.[60]

The other side of the story is the effect of low human development on India's economic growth. The impact of educational performance on growth performance is as marked in India as in other developing countries. One study has estimated that a single additional year in the average education period undergone by the workforce would raise economic output by 15 per cent.[61] Whether or not this assessment is exaggerated, the linkage to which it draws attention goes some way to explaining the weaknesses which have emerged in India's economic reform programme. One reason for the modest achievement of this programme, and its inherent instability, is that shortages of skilled labour in more employment-intensive sectors act as a barrier to sustained growth and employment creation. In China and most of the rest of East Asia, the progression was different. Prosperity was built on the foundations of labour-intensive manufacturing, where the expansion of employment helped to increase employment opportunities and incomes for the poor. But these improvements were premised upon increased productivity and the adoption of new technologies, which in turn required higher levels of skill. The crucial point is that the redistribution of opportunity in favour of the poor through public investment was a pre-condition both for grasping the opportunities provided by market-based growth, and for sustaining growth.

Widening inequalities in East Asia

The strong correlation between equity and growth in East Asia points to important lessons for policy makers in Latin America, Africa, and South Asia. It also suggests the need for reflection in East Asia itself, since inequalities are widening at an alarming rate in some countries of the region. In 1978, when China began its surge in economic growth, it was among the most equal countries in the world, with a Gini coefficient of

0.28. Today, its Gini coefficient stands at 0.39.[62] (See Figure 7.) This is lower than in Latin America, Africa, and most of East Asia, but the trend towards inequality is accelerating at a rate which is unprecedented in recent Chinese history, and unmatched in almost any other country for which reliable data is available (although Britain comes close). Rural-urban inequalities account for about half of the increase in inequality since the mid-1980s, and regional disparities for a further one-third. Government policies are exacerbating these differences.[63] In the social sector, public spending favours urban populations over rural, with the result that access to health care, education, and social welfare provision has become less equal. More broadly, economic policies continue to favour coastal over interior areas. As differences in access to health care, education, and economic opportunity become mutually reinforcing, the threat to future growth and human development will increase.

Similar patterns are emerging elsewhere. Inequality has been increasing rapidly in Thailand, with the Gini co-efficient increasing from 0.35 in 1975 to 0.45 in 1992.[64] As in China, marked regional disparities have been driving this trend, with the north-east falling further behind Bangkok and central regions. Intersecting with regional inequality has been inequality in educational achievement. According to the World Bank, the importance of education as a determinant of inequality has

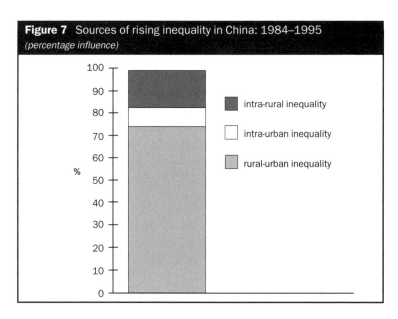

Figure 7 Sources of rising inequality in China: 1984–1995
(percentage influence)

increased by a factor of three since the mid-1970s, to account for 35–39 per cent of overall inequality in household income in 1992.[65] The urban-rural and inter-regional income divide has also become significantly wider. In fact, all of these elements reflect the emergence of a highly concentrated and increasingly sophisticated manufacturing sector, where the gap between returns to skilled and unskilled labour is increasing. These transformations are of broader policy relevance. For instance, development strategy in both Vietnam and the Philippines stresses the importance of attracting foreign capital to raise productivity, and in both countries manufacturing growth and foreign investment is highly concentrated. Governments concerned with the linkages between growth, equity, and human development need to ensure both a wider distribution of employment opportunities at higher levels of productivity, and increased access to education.

The debate about the relationship between growth and poverty reduction will inevitably continue to provide employment opportunities for economists worldwide. In a sense, however, the debate is only of marginal relevance. What East Asia's experience underlines is that, at the very least, growth *can* be successfully built on the foundations of improved equity and poverty reduction. There is no necessary trade-off between growth on the one side and equity and poverty reduction on the other. While cause and effect may be arguable, East Asia's experience suggests that there is a positive association between growth and equity.

Growth through redistribution

Policies for growth and poverty reduction are mutually reinforcing, rather than contradictory. This is because widespread poverty represents a vast waste of productive potential, reducing output and productivity, limiting the scope for savings and investment, and restricting market opportunities. Simply put, poverty represents not only a denial of basic rights but a source of economic inefficiency.[66] Overcoming that inefficiency should be a central policy objective for all governments.

Redistributive social and economic policies are vital to the achievement of this objective. In the past, debates about distribution have tended to focus narrowly on income. When it became apparent some three decades ago that the 'trickle-down' of wealth generated by growth was not happening in most countries at rates sufficient to make a dent in poverty levels, the World Bank elaborated a new approach under the banner of 'redistribution with growth'. The aim was to identify policies which resulted in poor people receiving a growing share of increments to national income. The redistribution of income was seen as the key to poverty reduction.

Here, we argue for a more integrated approach. Income distribution patterns are important, but they are the end result of the distribution of opportunities for production, employment, health care, and education. One of the reasons that patterns of income distribution are more equitable in East Asia than elsewhere is that countries in the region have achieved a wider dispersion of opportunities in each of these areas, which has fuelled economic growth. The contrast with other developing regions helps to explain some of the differences summarised in Figure 3. For instance, land distribution in most of East Asia is far more equal than in other regions. As a result, poor rural producers have had access to one of the productive assets needed to take advantage of market opportunities and contribute to economic growth, which has in turn been strongly correlated with poverty reduction.

Countries where land ownership patterns are highly unequal have suffered on both counts. Taking the 15 countries with the most unequal distribution of land, World Bank figures indicate that two have sustained growth rates in excess of 2.5 per cent a year — an abysmal performance.[67] More recent research has confirmed the negative impact of concentrated asset ownership for growth and poverty reduction in Latin America. According to the IDB, asset distribution has been the single most significant influence on growth in the region, retarding overall performance by about 2 per cent a year.[68]

Inequality in land ownership is one form of distribution which skews the benefits of growth against the poor. Another is inequality in opportunities for employment. In East Asia, the rapid growth of manufacturing industries has been associated with a high rate of job creation. Industrial development has been employment-intensive, and has also been associated with rising real wages. In Latin America and much of sub-Saharan Africa, by contrast, manufacturing growth has tended to be capital-intensive. In the 1990s, Latin America, in particular, has witnessed the emergence of 'jobless growth', with an expansion of manufacturing output being associated with a decrease in employment. Low-productivity (and low-pay) employment has increased the most, accounting for over 80 per cent of the jobs created in the 1990s.[69] The unemployment rate for the region as a whole has been rising uninterruptedly since 1989, despite the recovery in economic growth, reaching 8 per cent in 1995. Accompanying this trend has been a decline in real wages, with the result that poverty-in-employment has been increasing. In 13 out of 17 countries examined by the Economic Commission for Latin America, real wages were lower in 1995 than in 1980. Today, a waged job in the formal sector is no guarantee of an escape from poverty. In fact, a high proportion of the poor (more than 40 per cent in several countries) are to be found among wage workers.[70]

The structural factors behind growth with inequality are strengthened by differences in access to health care and education. Poor health and low skills are important factors in reducing the productivity of the poor and hence their capacity to participate in the economy on equitable terms. As we show in Chapter 3, East Asia has pursued public investment policies which have benefited the poor, while public spending patterns in much of Africa and Latin America have contributed to the exclusion of the poor from economic life.

In this book we argue that East Asia demonstrates the potential of a new development paradigm. The policy package associated with this paradigm can be summarised under the heading 'growth through redistribution', turning the old formulation on its head. Creating wealth on the foundation of highly unequal social and economic structures in the vague hope that the poor will ultimately benefit, has been tried, tested, and failed as a development strategy. The more effective strategy is to create an environment for poverty reduction and growth by redistributing assets and opportunities to the poor, enabling them to produce their way out of poverty.

3 Prioritising human development: the social policy fundamentals

'Get the macro-economic fundamental right and all else will follow.' This refrain is commonly heard in development debates, but it is based on false premises. Although good macro-economic policies are needed to create the material wealth to meet human needs, the extent to which those needs are met depends on the distribution of opportunities for production and employment — issues to which we now turn.

There is a two-way link between growth and human development. Education supports growth by enhancing skills, productivity, and adaptability. Meanwhile, healthier and better-educated people are capable of being more productive. The links can be mutually reinforcing, creating a virtuous circle, whereby increased growth generates resources for investment in health and education, which in turn fosters economic growth. Conversely, inadequate or poor quality investment in health and education slows growth and thus reduces the flow of resources available for public investment. Policies in East Asia have established strong positive linkages between growth and human development, serving to indicate the directions for policy reform in other countries. But complacency is unwarranted; there have also been major policy failures, and there are disturbing signs of past gains being rolled back, with access to health and education becoming less equal.

Lessons, and cautionary tales, from East Asia

Prioritising primary education

Long before theories of growth which recognised the importance of human capital became fashionable, there was a clear awareness in East Asia of the linkages between social and economic policies. Another central feature in East Asia's approach was the sequencing of investment in human development and economic growth, so that rapid progress was made towards achieving universal literacy and improved public health *in advance* of high growth. This meant that poor people were better equipped to respond to market opportunities as they emerged — and that they were able to claim a larger share of the benefits. It also meant that growth was built on the solid foundation of increasing skills levels, enabling productivity gains to be converted into rising real wages.

South Korea set a trend which other countries followed. In the early 1950s, only 13 per cent of the population had any formal schooling. Fifteen years later, over half of the population had been to primary school and 20 per cent to secondary school. Over the next 30 years, on average, five years was added to the time spent in school by children.[71] There were also huge advances in teaching quality, with Korean children now achieving some of the highest scores on scholastic tests.

There are important lessons to be learned from Korea about the financing of education, and about its potential benefits. The country started from a low base; in 1960, it was still a poor country which was heavily dependent on foreign aid. That aid, provided by the US, financed a large proportion of the initial primary-school extension programme. Thanks in part to this early investment in education, Korea was able to generate the growth which reduced its dependence on aid. The lesson: good aid works. In this case, it created the conditions for growth, increased self-reliance, and reduced dependency. As we suggest below, an international investment in getting Africa's children back to school through increased aid for educational provision could have similar effects, with benefits for recipients and aid donors alike. However, Korea's advance was not achieved by aid alone. Because the benefits of growth were equitably distributed, and because the benefits of education in terms of employment and incomes became increasingly apparent, parents were willing and able to meet a large part of the cost of secondary education, while public finances were concentrated on primary education. Equity in access to education has been one of the reasons for the high levels of equity in income distribution which have been main-tained during Korea's economic boom. By extending access to education beyond a small elite to the majority of its people, South Korea has reduced the premium that those with higher education enjoy over the rest of the population, leading to reductions in wage inequality. By contrast, in Brazil, education policy has remained geared towards an elite, with the poor quality of primary education reinforcing the privileges of wealthier groups and driving up inequalities.[72] The divergence between the two countries is striking. in the 1950s, the primary education completion rate in Brazil was almost twice as high as in Korea (60 per cent compared to 36 per cent). Over the next three decades, the position was reversed, with Brazil's primary completion rate falling to 20 per cent and Korea's rising to over 90 per cent.

South Korea powerfully demonstrates the positive linkages which can be established between growth and education. Other countries in the region have also been aware of the crucial role of investment in education. One of Indonesia's greatest achievements has been the spread of basic education opportunities. In the early 1960s, only one-third of children attended primary school. The proportion doubled over the next decade to 60 per cent by 1973 — higher than in India or sub-Saharan Africa today.[73] Enrolment is now almost universal, and the illiteracy rate has fallen to 15 per cent, from over 50 per cent in the late 1960s. These achievements were the result of an effort to increase the quality and quantity of services provided and — critically — to improve the access of poor people to those services. During the 1970s, the country embarked on a major drive to achieve universal enrolment, abolishing fees for primary schools, expanding the teacher-training programme, and building new schools. By the mid-1980s over 90 per cent of school-age children were in school.[74] As in South Korea, external support was a major factor in Indonesia's social development programmes, accounting for over half of spending in the first five-year development plan (1969–1974), after which economic growth and oil revenues enabled the country to increase its own investments.[75]

Beyond primary education: Indonesia and Thailand

Improved access to primary education was one of the foundations for East Asia's success, providing people with the basic literacy needed to raise skills. However, the view that primary education is the single most important determinant of growth with equity is misleading. As production systems develop, they demand higher levels of skill in order to sustain employment growth and rising incomes. This in turn requires that governments develop education systems which enable their citizens to climb the skills ladder. Universal primary education is the first step, but ignoring secondary education can be bad for growth and equity. The contrasting experiences of Indonesia and Thailand illustrate the point.

During the 1980s, Thailand's economy grew faster than that of Indonesia. However, the rate of decline in the incidence of poverty was so slow in Thailand that by the end of the decade there were more people below the poverty line than there had been in 1980. In Indonesia, by contrast, the number of poor people fell from 47 million to 27 million. The fact that the average per capita income in Indonesia was only half of that in Thailand makes the difference in performance even more striking.[76]

Differences in educational provision help to explain the apparent anomaly. Although both countries had achieved universal primary education in the 1970s, in Thailand enrolment growth at the lower secondary level was very slow and at the upper secondary level it was negative. In 1990, there were over 130,000 fewer pupils in secondary school than at the start of the decade, and the percentage of the labour force with only a primary education was higher for Thailand than for any other country in East Asia.[77] As the needs of the manufacturing sector shifted from a low-skills to a higher-skills workforce, employment opportunities for people with only a primary education stagnated, while those for people with a secondary education expanded. Since the poor were heavily under-represented in secondary education, from which they were excluded by cost, the impact of growth on poverty reduction was thus weakened, while wage inequalities increased.

More recently, there is evidence of a skills-shortage acting as a constraint on growth in both Indonesia and Thailand. This points to a future problem for the region. As economies move up the technological ladder, school leavers and adults with only a basic education will have a diminishing prospect of finding work in faster-growing and higher-wage sectors, with the wages of the unskilled falling progressively further behind those of the skilled. These problems are already evident in Thailand. After Chile, Thailand experienced the fastest-growing gap between the bottom and top ends of the labour market. This gap expanded by 50 per cent between 1987 and 1991, compared to 5 per cent in Indonesia, where the government prioritised spending in lower secondary education.

Progress and problems in China and Vietnam

One of the most important lessons from East Asia is that poverty is no barrier to rapid improvement in human development. In the 1950s, probably fewer than one in five people in China and Vietnam were literate. By 1980 the figure had climbed to two in three. Today, literacy rates are around 90 per cent — comparable to those of middle-income countries in Latin America.

Progress in the health sector was equally dramatic. By the end of the 1970s, China's rural co-operative health system covered about 85 per cent of the population, with a clinic in almost every village. There were about 1.6 million 'barefoot doctors' in place, or one to every 400 rural inhabitants — a higher doctor-to-patient ratio than in Canada in 1996.[78] Admittedly, coverage was not uniform and the quality of service provided was limited and variable. But the availability of basic medical care and immunisation, and a strong emphasis on preventative practice, contributed significantly to improvements in public health. Modelled on China's system, Vietnam's communal health-centres and village health-workers covered 90 per cent of the population by the mid-1970s.[79] Once again, services were variable in quality and often unresponsive to public need, especially the needs of women. But the incidence of killer diseases, such as diphtheria, tetanus, and polio, fell dramatically during the 1970s and 1980s, contributing to improved life-expectancy.[80]

Progress in health and education has not been achieved without setbacks, and immense challenges remain. In Vietnam, the public health system was chronically under-financed in the 1980s, leading to short-ages of drugs and poorly motivated staff. When the health system was liberalised in 1986 many people decided to opt out of the public health system and transferred *en masse* to private health pharmacies.[81] Attendance at public clinics has fallen by half since 1989, with a parallel shift towards self-prescription. Private spending on health is now some five times higher than public spending.[82] Moreover, cost-recovery has been introduced for government clinics, which are being financed increasingly by patient contributions and drugs charges. One result is over-prescription, as clinics seek to maximise revenue; another is the exclusion of poor people, who face difficulties in paying for health care.[83]

The challenge of poverty reduction remains immense, and it is becoming more difficult as poverty becomes increasingly concentrated in remote geographical areas, and in zones not linked to the centres of growth. In China, the absolute numbers involved are huge. More than 2 million children are not in school, 70 per cent of them girls.[84] Maternal mortality rates in interior districts are over 202 per 100,000 live births, well over twice the national average.[85] Meanwhile, for all the country's success in providing basic health services, it has been less efficient in preventative interventions. As many as 130 million people lack access to safe water, increasing their exposure to disease.[86] This sobering picture underlines the scale of the task ahead. That task will be made more difficult by the increasing concentration of poverty in more remote areas and by the gender discrimination which is undermining opportunities for girls and women. There is an added danger that the gradual shift towards more market-oriented systems of social sector financing will limit the access of poor people to basic services, leading to a widening health and education gap.

Health in China: The threat to equity

One of the most serious problems accompanying China's economic success has been a slow-down — and, in some areas, a reversal — in health care performance. Questions of improving access, providing finance, and raising efficiency now loom large on the policy horizon.

Prior to the economic reforms of the 1980s, access to health care was not equal. Provision in towns, much of it financed through a security health-care system applied to employees in state-owned enterprises, was generally better than in rural areas; and more prosperous rural areas were able to purchase better services than poorer ones. Even so, most of the population enjoyed access to basic services. On the eve of the reform programme, the rural co-operative health-care system, based upon collective funds and small individual contributions, covered about 85 per cent of the population.[87] Moreover, China provided an exceptionally large proportion of its population with risk-sharing coverage for catastrophic health care in hospitals. All of this was achieved through the investment of a relatively small share of GDP — around 2 per cent of the total in the 1980s taking into account government and private spending — in health care. The health outcomes resulting from this expenditure were exceptionally good. By 1990, life-expectancy — a highly sensitive indicator for overall performance — was five years longer than for a typical country at China's income level.

Threats to this achievement derive from a number of sources. Since the early 1980s, China's health system has come under increasing financial and administrative pressure. Budget spending on health has declined sharply as a proportion of GDP, from 0.8 per cent in the mid-1980s to 0.5 per cent today, in line with a broader decline in the weight of public spending in the economy (now one-third of the developing country average).[88] The most dramatic financial changes have resulted from the decline of the rural co-operative system, which began to break down after 1978. This left a major financing gap, with the share of health spending contributed by the co-operative medical system falling from 20 per cent of the total to less than 2 per cent over the 15 years from 1978. Spending on health care by the government also fell dramatically, from 32 per cent of the total budget to 14 per cent, between 1986 and 1996. Out-of-pocket payments have increased to fill the resulting gap in health financing. In 1978, direct payments by households represented 20 per cent of health sector revenue. The figure is now over 40 per cent.[89]

In addition, health provision in China is increasingly hospital-based and curative in orientation, with hospitals absorbing over three-quarters of total spending. These profound shifts in health financing have had important implications for equity in access to health services. Among the more significant indicators are the following:

- In the late 1970s, when rural collectives still operated, four out of five people had access to government health facilities. That figure has now fallen to one in ten.[90]

- Only 21 per cent of the total population is covered by risk-sharing insurance arrangements. Virtually none of the poorest-fifth income group are covered by risk-sharing schemes — and this group accounts for only around 5 per cent of total health spending.[91]

- Funding for the Epidemic Prevention Service, which has brought dramatic benefits in terms of reduced vulnerability to tuberculosis, diphtheria, tetanus, polio and measles, has fallen slightly in per capita terms since the mid-1980s.[92]

Two further factors have widened the gap between rich and poor in terms of health care. First, fiscal decentralisation has limited the capacity of governments to maintain equity in the health system, since the poor are concentrated in provinces and areas with more limited capacity to raise revenue. Second, the growing importance of government health insurance (which covers public sector employees) and enterprise-based insurance schemes as a mechanism for health financing, have resulted in urban areas being better provided for than rural areas. These two schemes represent 36 per cent of total health spending but cover only 15 per cent of the population. Their operation helps to explain why urban dwellers, who account for one-third of the total Chinese population, absorb over two-thirds of total health spending.[93]

Since health insurance coverage has virtually collapsed in rural areas, most services provided are fee-based. For poor households, the choice is often between purchasing health services at the cost of increased poverty, or forgoing health services and facing the risks associated with sickness. The impact of cost on use of health services has been underlined by recent surveys. One study in Xunyi county found that 42 per cent of households in the poorest income group reported illness but did not seek treatment.[94] In over half the cases, cost was cited as the reason for not seeking medical care. The same study found that poor households were far less likely to make use of inpatient services, with some 94 per cent of individuals (compared to 50 per cent for high-income groups) giving cost as the main reason. Given that the average cost of inpatient treatment amounted to 15 per cent of average household income and 60 per cent of the income of the poorest households, such findings are hardly surprising. The very high level of cost compared to income also has important livelihood implications. About 50 per cent of low-income households report having to borrow money to pay medical bills, with interest repayments severely reducing future income availability. Another study in Zhejan province notes that over 40 per cent of families living below the poverty line cite the cost of medical care as the most important contributory factor.[95] A particular concern from a public health perspective is an increase in revenue collection from immunisation services.

Shifting patterns of health financing have deepened inequalities between households, between rich and poor regions, and between towns and the countryside. Differences between provinces are especially pronounced. In the interior provinces of north, north-west, and south-west China, infant mortality rates are significantly above the national average, ranging from 60 to 80 deaths per 1000 live births in Guizhou and Qinghai respectively, to less than 20 deaths per 1000 births in Guangdong. In Guangdong, public health spending per capita has risen by over 2 per cent per annum since the early 1980s, whereas in poorer states such as Guizhou the increase is less than 0.5 per cent per annum.[96]

Growing inequity appears to be a major factor behind China's faltering human development performance. Child mortality rates are a particularly sensitive indicator for human development, since they reflect access to health care, access to water and sanitation, nutritional status, and overall poverty. Spectacular advances were achieved in the past: child mortality rates were halved from 173 to 85 deaths per 1000 live births from 1960 to 1975, and almost halved again by 1985 to 44 deaths per 1000 births. Since then, they have risen slightly.[97]

The Government of China responded in 1994 by initiating a project aimed at re-establishing the rural co-operative medical system in 14 counties with a high incidence of poverty. Community contributions, linked to ability to pay, have been introduced. These are topped up by contributions from government. However, it is envisaged that the largest share of financing for recurrent budgets at the facility level will come from payments for treatment and drugs. One of the problems which has emerged is that clinics are tending to over-provide costly services for drugs and treatment for those who can afford to pay, while failing to provide services for those who cannot.[98]

Without more radical reforms, the new programme is unlikely to address the deepening crisis in China's health structure. Five elements would appear to be crucial:

• The Chinese Government needs to identify, through local participation, the health services needed to address the most pressing problems facing the poor. These services would include preventative outpatient care, outpatient and inpatient care for the most basic diseases, and free child and maternal health care. Infectious diseases which pose a public health hazard should be included under this category.

• The health financing system needs to be reformed so that clinics are no longer rewarded for providing inappropriate high-cost services, but for providing low-cost preventive care. At present, the latter is financed by charges for the former.

• More effective social insurance provisions are needed so that the government can meet the health costs of those unable to pay.

• Drug use should be rationalised in the interests of reducing cost and improving efficiency. The present system, under which health facilities can increase their incomes by selling more drugs, should be abandoned. Clinics could be authorised to prescribe a small range of essential drugs, with any revenues from drug sales paid directly into community insurance funds rather than facility accounts.

• More emphasis should be placed on preventative care. This applies most immediately to reducing smoking, which claims over 800,000 lives a year as a result of chronic lung disease, cancer, and coronary disease. On present trends this figure will rise dramatically to over 2 million by 2025.[99] The costs to the health system will be immense; the treatment of smoking-related disease already absorbs 20 per cent of the government budget. Taxation on tobacco allied to a ban on advertising is vital if the effects of smoking on health are to be contained. More generally, the high public health costs of pollution (see Chapter 6) could be reduced through taxation and other measures, thereby releasing funds for low-cost preventative health care and the re-financing of the Epidemic Prevention Service.

Vietnam: The limits to a good example

As in China, health policy in Vietnam has prioritised primary health care provision through the communal health system (CHS). The CHS was not without its problems. It was underfunded, many of its staff were poorly trained, and services were often of poor quality. Despite these problems,

Vietnam was widely — if exaggeratedly — seen as a model for primary health provision in poor countries by the end of the 1970s.

Following *doi moi*, major changes and challenges have emerged in the health system. Private practice was legitimised, state control of the pharmaceutical industry was relaxed, and user fees were introduced in the public sector for drugs and services. The proliferation of private health provision confirmed a lack of public confidence in the quality of public health care. Health users voted with their feet, transferring to the private sector or resorting to self-treatment. By 1991, private-sector providers were seeing five times as many patients as public-sector providers.[100] The most striking trend has been that towards self-prescription, which is now the course of action adopted by two-thirds of people experiencing illness. According to the United Nations, private spending on health now accounts for 85 per cent of total health spending — one of the highest rates in the world.[101]

While the expansion of private-sector provision can be seen as an example of markets working to address public health problems, it could be interpreted as evidence of the need for more effective public health interventions. What is clear is that serious problems of equity and efficiency now confront the Vietnamese government.

Access

In February 1996 Oxfam GB carried out field research in communes in the north-central coastal province of Ha Tinh, one of Vietnam's 18 low-income provinces, to review the impact of *doi moi* in health and education.[102] The research revealed that utilisation rates for public health facilities dropped between 1990–1992, but they rose again in 1993 and have continued to recover since. Rising incomes among the poor, improved availability of drugs (albeit at a higher price), and improved management have all played a part. However, the study drew attention to the highly vulnerable position of poor communities, and to the damaging implications of user-charges for productive investment and savings activity among poor households. At a national level, 25 per cent of the poorest quintile of households reporting untreated illness cite financial considerations as the reason for not attending a health facility.[103] Poor households have faced increasing financial problems relating to health. In one survey, over one-third of poor rural households reported being forced to borrow in order to meet health costs. Paying for health care was cited as the most common reason for borrowing, ahead of paying for livestock or school fees.[104] Such accounts illustrate the way in which health costs can have adverse effects on rural livelihoods by diminishing savings and incomes, while increasing exposure to risk.[105]

Regional differences

As in China, there are marked regional differences in health status in Vietnam. In better-off provinces such as Haiphong, infant mortality rates are similar to those in countries such as Mexico and Thailand, where incomes are far higher; in the northern and central uplands, rates are closer to those of Bangladesh.[106] Regional differences also appear in other indicators, such as measles and malaria. If health provision is linked, through the private market, to ability to pay, regional inequalities will inevitable widen, reinforcing the widening income gaps between more prosperous and poorer areas.

Curative and preventive balance

The public health sector allocates a very low proportion of its budget to prevention. According to the World Bank, over 90 per cent of state budget expenditure is directed towards this end, with only 2 per cent spent on communal health stations and 5 per cent spent on preventative measures.[107] This high ratio is not consistent with the development of a more equitable and efficient health system which is responsive to public needs.

Health financing and drugs over-use

The growing consumption of drugs in a largely unregulated market is a threat to cost-effectiveness in health, as it is in China. Similarly, fee-for-payment provision inevitably leads to cost-escalation. More effective regulation of private pharmacies, and the creation of new financial incentives to reward preventative action, would appear essential. So, too, would the provision of free public services to treat the most basic infectious diseases.

Developing the public sector

Private sector medicine has filled a gap. However, a situation which results in 85 per cent of people by-passing formal health centres, and self-prescribing without adequate diagnosis, is not likely to contribute to Vietnam's impressive human development performance. Improving the quality of public health facilities through improved resources, better training, and the development of services responsive to local needs, would lead to more cost-effective patterns of drug utilisation and more equitable health outcomes.[108]

Learning from a bad example: the Philippines

The Philippines serves as a reminder of the costs of inappropriate policy priorities. During the 1980s, the Philippines spent comparatively less than other East Asian countries on health. In the 1990s, health spending has increased. But only one-quarter of the budget goes to the primary

health care system, which is most heavily utilised by the poor.[109] The result is that 30 per cent of the country's population — 23 million people — have no access to health facilities. In areas such as the Cagayan Valley and Southern Mindanao, where the incidence of poverty rises to over 40 per cent, less than half of the population has access to health facilities, exacerbating the vulnerability of poor communities.[110] Regional differences in health provision reinforce the effects of poverty. The National Capital Region of the Philippines accounts for over two-thirds of the country's spending on health. Ranked on the UNDP's Human Development Index, the region would be in the high development category, ranked 38. West Mindanao, one of the areas most poorly served by public health facilities, would be ranked next to Zambia at 136, with a life-expectancy ten years below the national average.

It is a similar picture in primary education. In theory, the Philippines achieved universal primary education at the same time as Korea. In practice, around one in three children who enter primary school do not complete it. Research carried out for Oxfam by a Philippines non-government organisation (NGO), the Freedom from Debt Coalition, graphically illustrates the discrepancy. In the urban municipality of Bocaue, around 85 per cent of all children enrol in primary school. However, of the girl children who enrol, only 4 per cent graduate.[111] Illness and cost were cited as the main reasons. Once again, under-funding is part of the problem. Despite having a higher per capita income than Indonesia, the Philippines spends less per capita on education. What it does spend is heavily skewed towards higher level facilities. In the tertiary sector, where most students can afford to pay, private spending by households has declined from 26 per cent to 22 per cent of public spending since 1986. In the primary sector, the share of households in overall financing has almost tripled, from 12 per cent to 31 per cent.[112] In effect, primary education is being financed by an increasingly regressive and heavily disguised system of taxation on poor people, diminishing access to schools for their children and reinforcing their poverty.

Quality and quantity in public spending

Why was East Asia able to make such rapid progress in social provision? Part of the answer is to be found in the linkage between growth and human development. In the 1970s, health spending in Latin America absorbed roughly the same proportion of GDP as it did in East Asia. Today, Latin America spends more of its national income on health. However, differences in growth mean that East Asia has tripled its spending over the intervening period, while in Latin America health spending has stagnated in real terms. It is a similar story in education Between 1970 and 1989, Korea quadrupled its spending on education in real terms, whereas Mexico's did not even double. This was not because of a difference in the percentage of GDP allocated to education, which declined slightly in Korea and rose in Mexico, but because of differences in the rate of economic growth. Other differences in social investment, notably in education, have contributed to differences in growth performance. According to some accounts, they are the single most important factor in explaining the divergence between East Asia on the one side, and Latin America on the other. For example, the IDB estimates that one-third of the growth gap between East Asia and Latin America can be traced to differences in primary school enrolment. Low levels of investment in schooling have also contributed to income inequalities in Latin America. In Korea, the rapid educational expansion of the 1960s and the 1970s led directly to reductions in the inequality of pay. By contrast, in Brazil education-relation shortages of skilled labour, allied to a slow rate of job creation, maintained high levels of equity. There is another negative 'feed-back loop' in play here. Poor educational performance reinforces poverty and inequality, which in turn act as barriers to entry to the educational system. According to one simulation, if Brazil were to achieve Korea's levels of income equality, it would increase secondary-school enrolment rates by over 20 per cent, with positive benefits for future growth and equity.[113]

For Africa, as for Latin America, the costs of under-performance in education have been high. One World Bank study concludes that variations in primary school enrolment rates are the main factor behind the differences in growth between East Asia and Africa. The methodology used may be open to question, but the high rates of return to investment in education are not in doubt.[114]

Economic growth is important to social policy because it provides the financial resources needed for investment. Without growth, it is difficult to sustain improvements in human development in the long term. During the 1980s, Zimbabwe invested heavily in primary education and basic health care, and achieved impressive results in terms of improved literacy and public health. For instance, adult literacy rose from 62 per cent to over 80 per cent and life-expectancy increased by five years. However, economic stagnation has contributed to a crisis in social-sector financing, starving the social sector of the resources needed to maintain progress. Per capita spending has fallen sharply in the 1990s, and the country's health and education infrastructure is coming under severe strain.[115] Health indicators in particular have started to deteriorate. What the Zimbabwean case demonstrates is that good social policy cannot substitute for macro-economic policy which sustains growth: neither is likely to succeed without the other.

Initial differences in income are insufficient explanation for the differences in performance between most of East Asia and much of the rest of the developing world. Growth has an obvious and important bearing on the capacity of states to deliver basic services. But the inadequacy of quantitative explanations can be demonstrated by comparing poorer countries in East Asia with counterparts elsewhere:[116]

• *China versus Bolivia:* In China, public spending on health is around $9 per capita, around half of the level of public health spending in Bolivia. With this smaller investment, China has achieved a maternal mortality rate which is one-sixth of that in Bolivia (115 compared to 650 per 100,000 live births), and an under-five mortality rate which is 20 per cent lower. In Bolivia, over one-third of the population does not have access to even the most basic health services. For China the comparable figure is 15 per cent.

• *Vietnam versus Uganda:* Spending on public health in Vietnam is around $1.5 per capita, compared to slightly under $3 per capita in Uganda. But Vietnam has health outcomes which are far higher than would be expected, based on international comparisons of countries at similar income levels. For Uganda the outcomes are worse than would be expected. The consequences are reflected in the fact that Vietnam's maternal mortality rate is 160 per 100,000 live births compared to over 1000 in Uganda, the child-mortality rate (45 per 1000 births) is 50 per cent lower, while almost twice as many of its citizens have access to health services.

• *Indonesia versus Brazil:* Public spending per capita on health in Indonesia is less than 10 per cent of that in Brazil. But Brazil's health system covers a smaller proportion of its population, and regional differences in public health are far wider than in Indonesia. Indonesia has a lower under-five mortality rate.

Such examples starkly illustrate the fact that the *quality* of public investment in human capital is as important as the quantity. Figures 8 and 9 capture the wide differences of equity in access to health care which separate countries in east Asia from Latin America. Thus while Vietnam's health spending is minuscule in relation to that of Brazil, it has achieved a higher level of access to basic services, which has in turn contributed to lower maternal and child mortality rates. Similarly, China

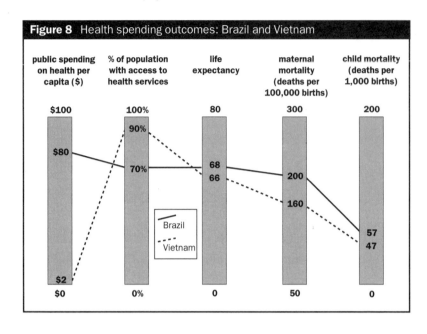

Figure 8 Health spending outcomes: Brazil and Vietnam

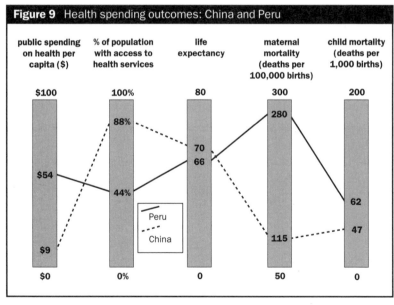

Figure 9 Health spending outcomes: China and Peru

has achieved twice the rate of coverage in its basic health services as Peru at one-sixth of the cost. Partly because of this higher level of service availability, China's citizens live longer, its children are less likely to die from infectious disease, and women in China are half as likely to die in childbirth. Of course, these differences in human welfare outcomes are determined by a far wider and more complex array of factors than access to public health services. But the importance of such services to the poor, who are often unable to afford private sector alternatives, can hardly be over-stressed.

However, quantity is also important. Most countries in sub-Saharan Africa and South Asia fall far below the levels of per capita spending in health and education needed to provide universal coverage for even the most basic services. For example, the World Bank has estimated the cost of a basic health package, capable of preventing or treating the diseases which account for the bulk of the disease burden for the developing world, at around $12 per capita. In India, primary health spending is slightly under $3 per capita, while most of sub-Saharan Africa falls in the range of $3–5 per capita. While improvements in efficiency are always possible, the need for increased spending is vital.

Prioritising the poor

Such examples illustrate one of the main social policy differences between East Asia and other developing regions: namely, each dollar of investment has tended to secure a higher rate of return in terms of human welfare. By comparison with other developing regions, East Asia has not been a big spender on social policy. Measured as a proportion of GDP, both Latin America and sub-Saharan Africa invest more than East Asia in health and education. (See Figures 10 and 11.) What is remarkable about East Asia is not that it spends so much, but that it spends so little. Of course, some countries in the region — such as South Korea and Taiwan — are spending a smaller part of a much bigger economic cake. But even when it was developing its social sectors in the 1950s and 1960s, the share of national income allocated to them was no higher than present levels.

The fundamental difference between East Asia on the one hand and Latin America and sub-Saharan Africa on the other, is that governments in the latter region have tended to concentrate resources on facilities such as universities and urban teaching hospitals, which are inaccessible to poor people. In the case of education, governments in East Asia

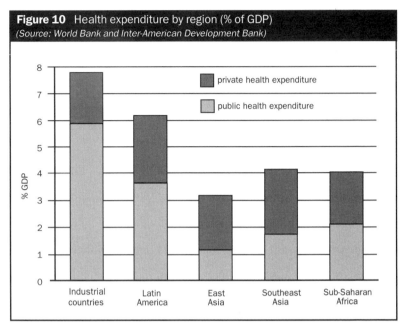

Figure 10 Health expenditure by region (% of GDP)
(Source: World Bank and Inter-American Development Bank)

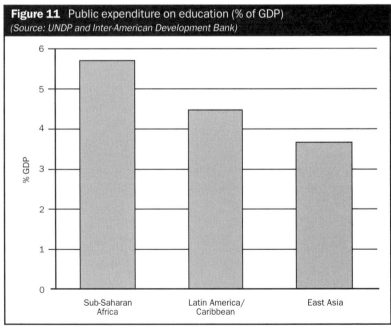

Figure 11 Public expenditure on education (% of GDP)
(Source: UNDP and Inter-American Development Bank)

typically allocate less than 10 per cent of their total budgets to the tertiary sector, with primary and lower secondary education absorbing over 85 per cent of education spending. Few governments in Latin America or Africa match this ratio. Most spend less than 70 per cent of their education budgets at the base of the schooling pyramid, with the result that a larger share of social-sector public spending is allocated to higher-income groups. To this basic inequity can be added a wide range of regional, social, and other inequities which result in poor people being excluded from access to health and education resources. These are considered below.

In the health sector, the differences in overall spending as a proportion of GDP summarised in Figure 10 provide an insight into one aspect of the social-policy differences between East Asia and other developing regions. Another difference concerns the balance between public and private spending. East Asia has a high level of private insurance spending, notably in South Korea. However, this is channelled through government-regulated health providers, with much of the finance coming through social insurance schemes. Higher levels of average income mean that individuals have more capacity to pay for health insurance. What is more striking is that almost half of health spending in sub-Saharan Africa, the region with the lowest average incomes, is private. For some in the World Bank, this high level of spending reflects the inherent superiority of private provision, and is an illustration of innovative copying of East Asia. In Oxfam's experience, it is simply the consequence of the catastrophic failure of the public health system to provide a service which meets needs. In most countries in the region, the rising costs of health care have placed services beyond the means of the poorest; a trend which has been reinforced by moves towards cost-recovery as an alternative source of health financing. In effect, this is a move towards regressive taxation, with poor people being forced to meet through private payments the costs of public services. As we suggest below, it is a move which poses major risks to public health. An important policy objective for Africa should be government financing of basic services, with a minimum package of preventative and curative interventions provided free at the point of entry to the system. We suggest below how the financing for such a package could be mobilised.

Bigger is not better

If living proof of the principle that 'bigger is not better' were required, it is duly provided by Latin America.[117] Only the OECD countries spend more of their national incomes on health. Yet despite these high levels of spending, most countries in Latin America have health outcomes well below the average for countries with similar income levels. An estimated 105 million people do not have access to formal health care — a fact which helps to explain why about one million children under the age of five die annually from preventable infectious disease. Each year, more than 2 million women give birth to children without having received ante-natal care. In Brazil, the most populous country in the region, one-third of the population has no access to health care. There are eight countries (Peru, Bolivia, Guatemala, Ecuador, Honduras, Haiti, El Salvador and Paraguay) for which that figure rises to 40 per cent or more.[118]

On the basis of international comparisons, the number of Latin Americans not covered by health systems is double what it should be. The resulting shortfall in provision costs lives. For the region as a whole, life expectancy should be 72 years rather than 69; mortality among children under the age of 5 should be 39 per 1000 live births rather than 47. This figure translates into the loss of around 100,000 child lives each year. Some of the region's most populous countries are among its worst performers:

- In Brazil, life expectancy is four years shorter than would be expected for a country with its per capita income, despite the fact that overall health spending absorbs 7 per cent of national income.

- Child mortality rates in Mexico are 20 per 1000 higher than would be expected, given the level of public spending on health. For Brazil and Bolivia the figure rises to 30 per 1000.

In education, as in health, Latin America's achievements fall far short of the minimum which should be expected — and still further short of those of East Asia. Net enrolment rates for primary school are high, at over 90 per cent. However, this masks the poor quality of education provided, and the fact that, on average, children spend only three years in primary school.[119] Repetition rates are the highest in the world. Using international comparisons again, the average period in education should be two years longer. Drop-out rates and repetition rates are high, so that fewer than half of the children who start primary school in any year finish it — and only one-quarter go on to secondary school.

Inappropriate priorities for public spending are part of the explanation for Latin America's under-performance. Countries such as Brazil, Mexico, Bolivia and — most spectacularly — Venezuela load their education budgets towards the tertiary sector. They each spend around one-half of their education budgets on basic education — a level which governments in East Asia would regard as totally unacceptable, and inconsistent with the attainment of high growth and employment creation. In the health sector, too, public spending in Latin America is heavily oriented towards high-cost, urban curative facilities, with liberal levels of subsidisation provided for private health insurance. Such facilities are of marginal relevance to the prevention and treatment of poverty-related infectious diseases suffered by the poor. As countries such as Vietnam and China have shown, major advances can be achieved in tackling such diseases through low-cost preventative measures and basic health provision at the community level.

Across Latin America, health care and education of high quality is readily available, but only to those who can afford it. Among the communities with which Oxfam's partners in the region work, in the slums of Brazil, the southern states of Mexico, and the Andean highlands of Bolivia and Peru, basic services are often non-existent. Indigenous communities, in particular, face extreme discrimination in terms of social-sector provision. In Bolivia and Mexico, children from these communities receive on average three years less education than other children. One of the main yardsticks for measuring equity in public policy is to consider the extent to which it acts to diminish regional differences in health outcomes. The scale of government failure in Latin America speaks for itself; regional differences in human development are extreme. In North-East Brazil, life expectancy is 17 years shorter than the national average, putting it on a par with Haiti. One-fifth of children in the region do not attend school, and illiteracy rates are double the national average.[120] Rural-urban difference also contribute to the human welfare gap between rich and poor. In Bolivia, rural infant mortality rates are 94 per 100 live births (compared to 58 per 1000 in urban areas), rising to over 170 in Andean Valley regions. Public policy has tended to exacerbate, rather than diminish, these differences by concentrating investment resources in urban areas.

Skewing budgets in India ...

Latin America demonstrates how the linkages between growth and human development can be weakened through poor social policies. While an extreme case, it is not alone. In India, over half of the combined budgets of states and federal government goes to curative health care, with a heavy bias towards urban areas. Another 15 per cent goes to the promotion of family planning, with scant regard for women's reproductive needs. There are also great discrepancies in per capita health spending between states, with the most impoverished, such as Bihar, Rajasthan, Madhya Pradesh, and Uttar Pradesh, receiving less than half the amount from central government than goes to wealthier states such as Punjab.[121] The systematic biases in favour of hospitals over primary health clinics, urban over rural provision, and contraception over women's health, is highly inefficient in relation to the needs of the poor. So, too, is a pattern of education spending which allocates less than 25 per cent of budget provision to the primary sector, despite adult illiteracy rates in excess of 50 per cent.[122] The costs of these spending patterns are reflected not only in the scale of social deprivation, but also in India's modest economic performance in comparison to countries in East Asia, with poor education acting as a brake on economic growth.

... and sub-Saharan Africa

Spending patterns in sub-Saharan Africa are equally disturbing. On virtually every human development indicator, the region is falling further behind the rest of the world. About three million children die annually from infectious diseases, most of which could be easily prevented through low-cost treatment. Maternal mortality rates are ten times higher than in East Asia and life expectancy is 20 years shorter. Perhaps most disturbingly of all in terms of future prospects, sub-Saharan Africa is now the only part of the developing world in which the number of children not attending primary school is increasing. By the end of the decade, an estimated 56 million 6–11 year-olds — over half of the total — will be out of school (see Table 1).[123] Of those who do enrol, probably more than one-quarter will leave before acquiring basic literacy skills.

Table 1: Children out of school *(Source: UNESCO)*

Region		1960	1980	1990	2000
Sub-Saharan Africa	Children (millions)	25	26	41	59
	Percentage	75%	43%	50%	51%
Latin America	Children (millions)	15	9	8	7
	Percentage	43%	18%	13%	11%
East Asia	Children (millions)	67	55	26	27
	Percentage	47%	25%	13%	12%

Unfortunately, instead of rising to the challenge of concentrating their limited investment resources in areas where they will produce the greatest social and economic gains, most governments prioritise investment in the wealthy. In Zambia, over 40 per cent of primary school children are not in the appropriate grade because of a lack of teachers, classrooms, and teaching materials. Yet less than half of the education budget is directed towards primary education. It is a similar story in Niger and Mali, where fewer than one-quarter of children attend primary school. In the health sector, most governments spend more than one-third of their budgets on central teaching hospitals, rising to around one-half in countries such as Uganda and Zambia. Together with the high levels of poverty prevailing in Africa, such priorities help to explain the dismal failure of health policy.

On a more positive note, the Ugandan government's poverty-reduction strategy provides a beacon of hope for sub-Saharan Africa. That strategy has prioritised the attainment of universal primary education.

Uganda: leading by example in primary education

In 1996 the government unveiled an ambitious plan to achieve universal primary education, announcing that free primary school places would be provided for up to four children from each household. The high cost of school fees has been a major deterrent to school enrolment and a cause of high drop-out rates. In the past, over one-third of children of primary-school age were not enrolled, while around one-quarter of those who were enrolled dropped out before completion, the vast majority before they could read or write.[124]

The positive results of the new policy are reflected in a rise in the number of children registered in primary school from 2.9 million in 1996 to 5.7 million in 1997.[125] However, success has brought with it enormous policy challenges. Doubling the primary-school-age population has also doubled the pupil-to-teacher ratio, to almost 80:1. One in three teachers are untrained; at least 40,000 new classrooms are needed urgently; and teaching materials are in short supply, with only one book available for every six children. The danger is that the quality of education provided in such over-crowded and ill-equipped classes can only be low, and the aim of providing high-quality universal education will not be achieved.

This danger can be averted. Donors have responded positively to the Ugandan Government's initiative, with the World Bank providing extensive support for classroom construction, teacher training, and educational materials. More could be done, notably by accelerating debt relief. Uganda was the first country to be granted debt reduction under the terms of the Highly Indebted Poor Country (HIPC) initiative. However, the rate of disbursement for debt relief will be slow.[126] Over the next few years debt relief will amount to around $20m a year, while debt repayments will exceed $160m — more than the government is spending on primary education. The World Bank and the IMF, who between them account for over two-thirds of the debt, will release funds over a period of 40 years and ten years respectively. 'Front-loading' debt relief, by implementing the HIPC framework over a five-year period, would release significant amounts of money, which could be invested in education. Donors and the Ugandan government could also co-operate in providing education incentives. One of the most effective would be a school-meals programme, with children being provided with free and nutritious meals. World Bank support for such programmes in Tamil Nadu in India, and in Niger, has contributed to increased enrolments (partly because of the reduced burden on households) and better educational performance, with children's learning capacity being improved along with their nutrition.

The Ugandan Government itself could do more. It has set a target for raising to 50 per cent the share of the national budget allocated to poverty reduction measures. However, high levels of unproductive expenditure are a barrier to progress. Over 5 per cent of national income, more than the entire education budget, is currently spent on parastatal subsidies.[127] Military spending is also high, and the social-sector budgets are skewed toward universities and teaching hospitals. Within the education sector there is an urgent need for innovation and decisive action. Double-shift teaching would help to reduce the pupil-to-teacher ratio, but it is imperative that targets for improved teacher-training and teacher recruitment are met. An emergency classroom construction programme is now under way, but this has slipped behind schedule as a consequence of bureaucratic delay.

Public access, financing, and quality of service

Consistent under-funding inevitably erodes the quality of services being provided, and hence the potential benefits to their users. In the case of education, poor households with limited resources inevitably weigh the costs of schooling against the perceived advantages it provides. School fees, uniforms, and teaching materials are the main direct costs, but there are also significant indirect costs, since children are an important source of labour. This applies especially to young girls, who are required to carry water, care for their siblings, and assist in the preparation of food. Where the educational facilities provided are inadequate, a household is less likely to invest scarce resources, and more likely to withdraw children from school, usually starting with girl children.

The poor quality of basic services provided to poor communities is evident across the regions in which Oxfam works. Among the most important causes of drop-out and repetition are poor infrastructure, low attendance, lack of textbooks and other teaching materials, and the lack of pre-primary education. In sub-Saharan Africa, a primary school is often a mud hut with a leaking roof, with classes of 40 children to one teacher, and a chronic shortage of basic teaching materials. In Mozambique, per capita spending on teaching materials is around 70 cents per pupil. The minimum package of books and pencils needed to provide an adequate basic education costs around $4. Inevitably, teaching quality suffers. Poor school maintenance and inadequate facilities are another powerful deterrent to attendance. In Honduras, only half of primary schools have access to safe water;[128] in poor areas of Peru, such as the Andean highlands where Oxfam works with rural communities, it has been estimated that only 2 per cent of schools have water, drains, and electricity. The resulting health risk to children leads to high levels of drop-out and non-attendance.

National data often exaggerate the quality of education. For instance, Mexico has achieved universal enrolment for primary schools. Literacy rates are estimated at around 90 per cent. However, the definition of literacy is a restricted one, and many primary schools in poor areas are ill-equipped to deliver basic skills. In the states of Campeche and Chiapas, where there is a high concentration of poverty, one-third of schools provide only three grades of instruction, so that the majority of children entering school leave without having acquired basic literacy and numeracy skills.[129]

In the health sector, too, the quality and location of service provision is a major barrier to entry. In the Kibale region of Uganda, Oxfam's partners work with one community for whom the nearest health facility is 18 miles away. One recent survey has shown that, even if it were closer, few people would use it. Drugs for the treatment of malaria (the main health problem) and other basic diseases are in short supply, and there is a perception that staff are poorly trained and disrespectful. On the staff side, poor morale is acknowledged as a serious problem. The problems are familiar across much of the developing world. Primary health care budgets have come under increasing pressure from a combination of factors, with slow growth and debt prominent among them. As in education, staff salaries have been cut dramatically, forcing medical personnel to take on other jobs, and training budgets have been cut. Such a situation is not conducive to the delivery of high-quality services.

Policy responses to problems in the financing and delivery of health and education have often had the effect of eroding the access of poor people to basic services. We will consider three such policies in more detail: structural adjustment, cost-recovery, and decentralisation.

Structural adjustment
These programmes are introduced to address financial crises which typically include problems of large budget deficits. In some cases, the resulting financial adjustment has fallen heavily on social-sector budgets. For sub-Saharan African countries undergoing adjustment reviewed by the World Bank, total social spending fell by almost 1 per cent of GDP, while the share of national budgets going into the social sectors fell from 25 per cent to 22 per cent.[130] In some cases, per capita spending cuts have been very high:[131]

- In Zimbabwe, per capita spending on primary health and primary education was cut by one-third from 1990 to 1995 under an IMF-World Bank adjustment programme.

- In Zambia per capita health spending fell by half between 1990 and 1994. Expenditure on primary school children is now less than half of the level of the mid-1980s

- In Tanzania, per capita health and education spending is one-third lower than the levels of the mid-1980s.

Inevitably, public spending retrenchments on this scale have undermined the quality of service provision. The burden has fallen most heavily on poor people, who are unable to afford private-sector services. Per capita spending cuts in government health budgets have been introduced at a time when increasing poverty, HIV-AIDS, and the emergence of more deadly strains of infectious disease are increasing the demands made on a shrinking system.

Cost-recovery and creeping privatisation
Recent debates over social-sector reform have been dominated by disputes over the respective roles of the market and the private sector. These debates can serve to obscure an important fact: namely, that

under-financing is encouraging a process of creeping privatisation, as households are forced to fill the gap left by shortfalls in public spending. In India, for example, much of the cost of health care — around three-quarters of the total — comes out of direct payments by households, with the proportion of household budgets accounted for by health spending having risen by a factor of seven since the mid-1960s.[132] In Zambia, it has been estimated that around 80 per cent of the costs of primary school education are met out of household budgets.[133] In both cases, real household outlays have increased as state provision has fallen. Inevitably, it is the poor, with the smallest income relative to costs, who suffer the heaviest burden. Evidence from several countries — including India — points to health-care costs as the main source of indebtedness among the poor.[134]

In addition to the privatisation of health and education financing by default, a growing number of governments have sought to shift the burden of funding away from state budgets on to households through a policy of cost-recovery, or charging for the services provided. The World Bank has been a vigorous, if slightly schizophrenic, advocate of cost-recovery, with its President expressing opposition to charges on basic services, but many of its programmes including recommendations in this direction.[135] Clearly, the impact of cost-recovery on equity will depend on which services are subject to charges. Fees for sophisticated curative treatments in hospitals, which are not used by the poor, will have a different impact from fees for immunisation, ante-natal care, and basic curative treatments in rural health centres. Similarly, households from which university students come are more likely to be able to afford university fees, than are poor households to afford charges for primary education.

While most governments and the World Bank profess their concern to combine cost-recovery with equity, insufficient attention has been paid to the social consequences of charging for basic services. In many cases, the cost to society of excluding poor people from basic services is high. For instance, diminished access to health services reduces productivity and increases general exposure to the risk of communicable diseases. Similarly, reduced educational attendance will erode the country's long-term potential for economic growth. This is why primary education and basic health services are 'public goods' for which all states should assume responsibility for providing to their citizens.

Cost-recovery policies have increased poor households' vulnerability to poverty, and undermined livelihoods. An illustration is the frequent and growing recourse to distress sales of productive assets in order to pay for health care. For instance, it has been estimated that 40 per cent of land sales in Kenya are a direct consequence of illness. By depleting their assets, poor households lower their future productive capacity, thereby increasing vulnerability to future health risks and diminishing the resources available for spending in other areas. More immediately, the effect of cost-recovery is to make basic services unaffordable to the poor:

- In Zambia attendance at one of the country's main teaching hospitals fell by half over the five years following the introduction of cost recovery in 1989. Participatory research carried out in 1995 concluded that: 'in all sites user-fees have continued to place the formal health system beyond the reach of the poor.'[136]

- User-fees were introduced in Zimbabwe in 1991. By 1993, the number of babies born whose mothers had not registered for ante-natal care had increased by 30 per cent. Mortality among these mothers was five times the national average.[137]

- In Kenya, the introduction of user-fees led to a sharp drop in attendance at clinics for the treatment of sexually transmitted diseases.[138]

As with health care, households have been required to meet a growing share of the costs of education out of private spending in the form of school maintenance fees and other charges; and the effect has been to exclude the children of the poorest households from schools.

Decentralisation
Decentralisation can have positive effects. It can locate the managers of basic service facilities closer to the users of services, making managers responsive to local needs. Political and financial decentralisation can also foster a sense of accountability, especially where there are opportunities for people to influence the appointment of office-holders. However, decentralisation can often have negative effects and potentially damaging unintended effects, widening inequalities in social welfare provision. This has happened in China, with the economic boom in coastal areas financing a sustained improvement in health services, while provision in interior areas has stagnated.[139] In Brazil, as in China, financial decentralisation has resulted in the transfer of responsibility for raising revenue to states and municipal governments, which now account for over 90 per cent of educational expenditure.[140] Per student educational spending now ranges from $130 in the poorest state of Piaui to $1000 in the richest state of Sao Paulo. This is despite the fact that

poverty incidence is around four times higher in Piaui. The effect of financial decentralisation in this case has been to widen the gulf in life chances between rich and poor. Spending in the three wealthiest states is now six times higher per pupil than in the poorest three states. Since income is growing more rapidly in the richer states, investment resources will, in the absence of redistributive mechanisms, become even more heavily concentrated on richer areas. Over the longer term, the effect will be to concentrate the benefits from economic growth increasingly heavily in the wealthier states, while diminishing the benefits to states with the highest incidence of poverty.

Some of the unintended effects can be illustrated by Uganda's experience, which has proceeded rapidly towards political and financial decentralisation. The recurrent budget for education is now financed out of a block grant allocated by government to district authorities, which have the power to determine priorities. However, it has been estimated that less than 30 per cent of this grant reaches schools.[141] The reason is partly corruption, but mainly that district authorities choose to construct rural feeder roads rather than schools. The two cases respectively illustrate that financial decentralisation needs to be accompanied, first, by redistributive measures, with the central government ensuring that poor regions do not lose out; and second, by measures to ensure effective and accountable implementation of national policy priorities.

Learning from East Asia: five policy guidelines

All countries face financial pressures in meeting needs for health care and education. Demand is potentially infinite and the supply of finance is limited. This is as true for the British National Health Service as for the health services in African countries. However, the tension between financial capacity and human need is far greater in developing countries. Viewed from a global perspective, the paradox is that countries with the highest incidence of illness and the greatest deficits in education have the most limited resources for addressing the problems. That said, almost all governments could do more, as could the wider international community. There are five main areas of policy where guidelines are needed:

Budget guidelines and composition of spending

There are no blueprints for either. Governments in countries with low levels of human development should probably aim to spend around 5 per cent or more of national income on education, and probably somewhat more than 2 per cent on health. More important is the quality and composition of spending, and the balance between private and public spending. Governments in East Asia have concentrated public investment resources at the primary level, while charging for higher-level facilities. For countries which are a long way from achieving universal primary education and access to primary health care, international evidence suggests that a target of between 80-90 per cent of education spending should be directed towards primary and lower secondary levels, and at least 70 per cent of public spending in the health sector should be directed to primary facilities and preventative measures.

Public spending for public goods

Private providers are not good at providing basic health and education services to poor people for one very obvious reason: poverty exposes people to high risk of illness and is associated with limited purchasing power. Creeping privatisation through cost-recovery similarly has the effect of excluding poor people from basic services. The costs of exclusion from basic health and education are high both for individuals and for society. In sub-Saharan Africa well over half of recurrent spending on health and primary education now comes out of people's pockets, rather than being financed by public investment. In both sectors the aim should be to shift the balance progressively between public and private finance. For health, the focus should be on the provision, through public spending, of a basic package of low-cost services to prevent and treat the most common infectious diseases, with free maternal and child health services. In education, the initial aim should be to provide free primary education. The task is immense. But Uganda, one of the world's poorest countries, is in the process of showing that it is not impossible.

Diverting wasteful expenditure into social investment

Wasteful expenditure takes a wide range of forms. Three merit especially urgent attention: military spending, corruption, and misplaced subsidisation.

Military spending

In South Asia, India and Pakistan have some of the world's most impressive military hardware, along with some of its most depressing social indicators. The two facts are related. India spends more on military capacity than it does on health — and Pakistan spends more in this area than on health and education combined. In Pakistan, the ratio of military personnel to doctors is 9:1. In India the ratio is lower, but still an appalling 4:1.[142] Successive governments in both countries have pointed to poverty and low average incomes as barriers to improving performance in social welfare provision. Such constraints have not, however, dampened enthusiasm for populist promises aimed at securing re-election. For instance, today's Indian Government is bound by a 50-year-old constitutional promise of insuring universal access to primary health care, and a more recent pledge to achieve universal primary education. Meeting the pledge on access to primary health services would cost, according to World Bank estimates, the equivalent of 0.3 per cent of GDP, or one-tenth of the country's military budget.[143] The trade-off between social provision and military spending is even more pronounced in Pakistan. This is a country which performs poorly on education, even in comparison with India. The overall literacy rate is 35 per cent (and 23 per cent for women). Only around one-half of the population has access to basic health services. Yet Pakistan's rulers are apparently convinced that they are able to afford to spend 25 per cent more on military hardware and personnel than they spend on health and education combined.

By international standards, governments in sub-Saharan Africa are modest spenders on arms. But they still manage to mobilise $14 per person — roughly double what they spend on health and education combined. Converting tanks into primary health services would be one of the most effective ways to advance human development. For example, in 1994 Nigeria took delivery of 18 Vickers tanks from the UK at a cost of $150m. For considerably less it could have provided full immunisation to the estimated 2 million children not currently covered. In Latin America, military budgets absorb a lower percentage of GDP than in any other developing region. That said, there are some extravagant exceptions. Peru, for example, has recently purchased a dozen Mig-29 fighters from Belarus a cost of $350m — roughly $2 per capita. This is considerably less than it spends on primary health care in the Andean highlands, where inadequate health provision poses a more immediate threat than aerial attack from neighbouring states.

Targets should be set for reducing military spending in order to finance priority social spending. On average, countries in sub-Saharan Africa and South Asia currently allocate 3 per cent or more of GDP to what is euphemistically described as 'defence'. The aim should be a ceiling of between 1 and 2 per cent. For sub-Saharan Africa, a 1 per cent reduction in military spending would release sufficient resources to double spending on health care.

Corruption
This is not the sole preserve of poor countries, but some of the poorest among them have developed it into an art form; and the costs of corruption in terms of lost opportunities for human development are far higher in poor countries. For example, the estimated $400m which Kenyan politicians have diverted into foreign bank accounts in recent years would finance the budgets for primary health care and primary education, with something to spare. Taking responsibility at the highest political level for ensuring greater transparency and accountability in public finance should be treated as an urgent political priority. National commissions charged with investigating and publicly reporting on evidence of corruption would be a step in the right direction.

Misplaced subsidisation
Public finances are often swallowed on a huge scale by loss-making parastatals, most of which provide limited employment to a small number of people at enormous cost. In Zimbabwe, subsidies to the loss-making National Iron and Steel Company have remained intact, while the health and education budgets have been heavily cut. This is despite the fact that the effects of these subsidies on employment creation are weak (amounting to around $100,000 per job), while the social-opportunity-costs of lost health and education spending are high. In Uganda, state subsidies to loss-making parastatals amounted to $270m in 1995, amounting to 5 per cent of GDP. This represented four times the amount spent in that year on education and five times the amount spent on health.[144]

Governments in all countries, rich and poor alike, face hard choices in public spending on social sectors. Demands for services inevitably outstrip financing capacity, with the result that rationing is needed. Inevitably, the rationing process is shaped by political influence in the development of public policy priorities. All too often, this influence results in patterns of resource allocation which are geared towards the interests of the rich and powerful, regardless of the costs to the poor, and the wider public interest. In India, the constraints on health and education spending outlined above are the consequence in part of decisions to subsidise agriculture. Over 8 per cent of GDP is spent annually in subsidies for credit, irrigation, electricity, and on public spending schemes for rural roads, extension and infrastructural projects. This compares with less than 5 per cent of GDP spent on health and education.[145] While public spending on agriculture brings important benefits to the poor in terms of employment and production opportunities, many of the subsidies are regressive, since it is the biggest farmers who receive the bulk of the benefits from subsidised access to fertiliser, power for irrigation, and credit. Striking a better balance between concentrating benefits on the poor and giving wider subsidies which disproportionately benefit the better-off is crucial.

Mobilising public finance through progressive taxation

Governments often claim that the universal provision of basic services is unaffordable because of limits on revenue-raising capacity. Structural adjustment programmes, which tend to recommend reduction in marginal income tax and corporate taxes, reinforce this view. The assumption in both cases is that high taxes are bad for growth. So, indeed, is the inadequate provision of basic services. In fact, the costs of meeting basic services is more modest than is often assumed — comprehensive primary health care coverage in poor countries, according to the World Bank, would cost about $12 per head. Meanwhile, the capacity of governments to raise revenues is less limited than is often assumed.

This is especially true of income tax in Latin America, for example. On average, governments in Latin America collect 14 per cent of their GDP in tax.[146] The comparable figure for East Asia is 16.8 per cent. Income differences alone cannot explain the discrepancy. Mexico has a higher average income than Thailand, but collects 2 per cent less of GDP in tax. Average income in Peru is twice that in Indonesia, but the government collects 3 per less of GDP in tax, despite grossly inadequate social investment levels. The problem is not solely one of low tax, but also of poorly targeted tax. In Latin America the incidence of taxation is heavier for the poor than the wealthy because of the level of dependence on consumption taxes. Taxes on income, property, and financial assets, where marginal tax increases are more progressive, are low. For example, Brazil collects less than 5 per cent of GDP in tax, which is half the level of Malaysia (which has a similar average income) and Indonesia (where average incomes are one-third lower). (See Figure 12.)

In some cases structural adjustment programmes have been accompanied by improved tax policies. In Uganda, better tax administration has enabled the government to increase the share of GDP collected as revenue from 5 per cent to 13 per cent since 1985. This has enabled it to finance an increase in spending on health and education while meeting its stabilisation targets for low inflation. In Zimbabwe, by contrast, reductions in corporate, commercial, and top income-tax rates lowered the collection of taxation by 3 per cent of GDP over the period 1990–1995 — an overshoot of targets agreed with the IMF.[147] The efficiency gains were questionable. Commercial farm land in particular is heavily under-taxed in Zimbabwe, leading to a poor allocation of resources as well as a loss of revenue for investment in social priority areas. The devastating impact of reduced investment in health and education on poor people in Zimbabwe, and the adverse consequences for long-term growth, suggest a misplaced sense of priorities, in which stabilisation targets have taken priority over investment in human capital.

Specific taxes can be developed to mobilise funds for social-sector provision. For instance, South Korea levies a small tax on interest and dividends to finance part of government spending on education. In countries such as Zimbabwe and Brazil, a similar tax on commercial farm-land would be good for both equity and efficiency, since a large area of productive land in both countries is unused.

Supportive international action

Development co-operation could play a central role in helping to meet targets for improving health and education in areas such as debt, aid, and military spending:

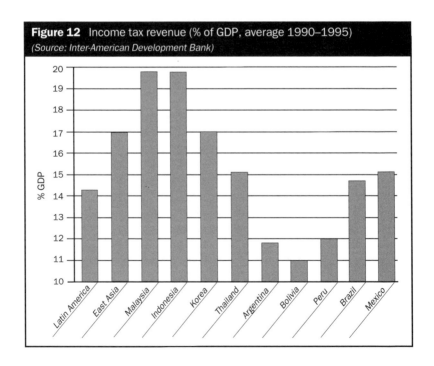

Figure 12 Income tax revenue (% of GDP, average 1990–1995)
(Source: Inter-American Development Bank)

Debt relief

Debt servicing is one of the heaviest burdens on budgets in poor countries. In countries such as Tanzania, Zambia, Mozambique, Honduras, and Nicaragua, debt repayments absorb more than one-fifth of total government revenue, dwarfing the amounts spent on primary health and education. In Mozambique, debt servicing will be absorbing over 40 per cent of Government spending by the year 2000 — some four times the likely level of spending on health and education.[148]

The Highly Indebted Poor Country (HIPC) debt initiative could help to resolve the debt crisis.[149] One problem is that the time-frame (six years for most countries) is too long, and the targets for debt sustainability have been set unrealistically high. Another is that no linkage has been established between debt relief and initiatives to promote human development. Oxfam International believes that the HIPC framework could be used to provide positive incentives for poverty reduction. Debtor governments who commit themselves to converting savings from debt into social priority investment should be rewarded with deeper debt relief and an accelerated time-frame. More specifically:

- debt relief should be provided within three years, rather than the six years currently stipulated;
- debt relief should be deepened to the range of 15-20 per cent for debt service (from the present 20–25 per cent range), and to 150–200 per cent for the debt stock to export ratio (from the present range of 200–250 per cent).

In this context, Oxfam International has proposed a debt-for-poverty-reduction contract under which debtor governments would be granted privileges on a conditional basis, the main condition being that they allocate funds in a transparent manner to achieve targets for improving human welfare.

International aid

In South Korea and Indonesia, aid initially played a crucial role in financing primary education. In time, improved access to education led to higher growth, improvements in human development, and reduced dependence on aid. Good aid, as this example demonstrates, improves self-reliance. At present, however, aid policy suffers from a lack of commitment to maintain spending, and from poor quality. Recent years have witnessed steep declines in aid spending. For the OECD countries as a group, development assistance has been reduced by 18 per cent in real terms since 1990 to its lowest level since the early 1950s — around

0.27 per cent of their combined GDP.[150] One area in which aid can bring the most tangible benefits is in carefully targeted social provision with a focus on poverty reduction and human development.

Unfortunately, most aid, like most government spending in poor countries, is poorly allocated. Education is the single largest sector, accounting for 10 per cent of total aid. Unfortunately, only 0.6 per cent goes to primary education. The share of health care in the OECD's collective aid budget has fallen to around 5-6 per cent, or around half the peak reached in the early 1980s.[151] International co-operation to get the world's children into school would be a highly effective use of aid, and sub-Saharan Africa an obvious place to start. Donors should set a target for doubling the share of aid allocated to primary education by the year 2000, which would release around, $28bn in new resources. Debt relief specifically linked to education provision could be used to mobilise further resources. In both cases, firm timetables should be drawn up for increasing school enrolments and reducing gender differences in enrolment. Allied to improved allocation in government spending, which should be a condition for support under the initiative, this would bring the targets agreed at the 1995 Social Summit within reach.

Arms transfers

Ultimate responsibility for excessive military spending rests with those who authorise it. However, those who supply the weapons are not blameless. More than four-fifths of all arms transferred are provided by permanent members of the Security Council. Action is needed to tackle the supply of arms, by the introduction of restrictive arms codes aimed at reducing the transfer of weapons, including small arms.[152] More generally, aid donors should seriously reconsider the wisdom of supporting governments which prioritise military spending over the health and education needs of their people.

4 Employment and manufacturing

East Asia's experience has been at the centre of a protracted debate about the role of the state in industrial development. Two competing models have emerged. The first is that of a minimalist state, in which the limited nature of government intervention has been stressed. General openness to trade, the minimal use of subsidies, and progress towards deregulation are regarded, in this view, as the hallmarks of the East Asian model. While the extensive nature of past state intervention is acknowledged, it is claimed that trade liberalisation, financial deregulation, and adherence to market signals have been the primary determinants of rapid growth.[153] The second model has stressed the central role of the state as a promoter of industrial development, with the use of trade barriers and control of investment.[154] East Asia is cited as a typical illustration of the former approach, and Latin America and Africa of the latter.

Reality is more complex. East Asian countries have adopted a wide range of industrial policies, which vary from case to case and over time. What they have shared in common is a commitment to achieving full employment, with rising real wages. Trade, investment, and industrial policies have been tailored to this objective, with state interventions aimed at optimising market outcomes and employment opportunities. Working towards full employment has been an explicit policy objective. 'Free markets', in the sense usually ascribed to industrial development in East Asia, have been conspicuous by their absence.

There have, however, been important differences between East Asia and other developing regions. Most developing countries combined illiberal trade and price policies with fiscal profligacy and over-valued exchange rates. The failure of this import-substitution model has often been attributed solely to micro-economic policy, whereas macro-economic and institutional failures were often more important.[155] In the case of East Asia, import restrictions have been central to East Asia's economic growth, contributing to the development of domestic capacity. While the short-term costs of such restrictions may have been high, they do not inherently create instability or reduce long-run growth, and the acquired comparative advantage which resulted brought considerable long-term benefits. Unlike other developing regions, East Asia did not, until recently, ally import protection to currency over-valuation. This combination inevitably results in trade deficits that are unsustainably large, and balance-of-payments crises. Similarly, subsidies to specific industries, whether in the form of credit, foreign exchange or support for innovation, can stimulate productivity and enhance long-term efficiency in other economic sectors (for instance, an efficient machine-tools industry can underpin growth in manufacturing). In a worst-case scenario (which would characterise much of sub-Saharan Africa, South Asia and parts of Latin America) industrial subsidies have produced rent-seeking activity, or been misdirected. But carefully targeted subsidies of the type which have been developed with varying degrees of success in East Asia, do not have the same destabilising effects as large-scale and sustained budget deficits (of the type, once again, which have figured prominently in Latin America and sub-Saharan Africa).

Manufacturing export growth

Various features of East Asia's success in manufacturing are well known. In the 1960s, South Korea and Taiwan achieved industrial growth rates in excess of 10 per cent a year. The second wave of 'tiger' economies — Indonesia, Malaysia, and Thailand — followed hard on their heels, making the transition from dependence on primary commodities to emerge as major manufacturing exporters. The share of manufactured exports in total exports has grown from less than 6 per cent in all three countries to 41 per cent for Indonesia, 61 per cent for Malaysia, and 77 per cent for Thailand. In the last 25 years, the share of the industrialised countries in global manufacturing value-added has fallen from 88 per cent to 80 per cent — almost all of this shift is accounted for by the rise of East Asian exports.[156]

Export growth has been central to the rise in living standards experienced across East Asia. (See Figure 13.) On a per capita basis, the value of exports has risen by 14 per cent a year in the 1990s, compared to a rise of 7 per cent for Latin America and a fall of 1.6 per cent for Africa. The difference is partly related to the composition of exports. Today, the share of manufactured goods in Africa's exports is less than 10 per cent, and dependence on primary commodities has hardly changed over the past three decades.[157] During the 1980s, deteriorating prices for primary commodities erased around 5 per cent of the value of regional GDP in

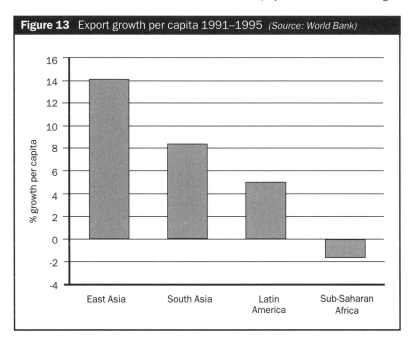

Figure 13 Export growth per capita 1991–1995 *(Source: World Bank)*

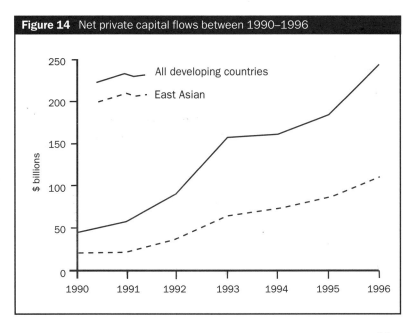

Figure 14 Net private capital flows between 1990–1996

sub-Saharan Africa. More broadly, dependence on exports characterised by low value-added has contributed to a situation in which the 44 Least Developed Countries, accounting for 10 per cent of the world's population, have seen their share of international trade shrink by half — to 0.3 per cent of the total — over the past decade.[158] Like sub-Saharan Africa, Latin America remains heavily dependent on primary commodities (which account for over one-third of export earnings), while its share of world manufacturing trade has stagnated at 4 per cent since 1970.

Success and failure in international trade have been major factors in explaining global trends in income and poverty. Because international trade has been growing faster than world output, it has acted as a dynamic engine of growth. East Asia has benefited because the region has successfully participated in global markets, so that the share of trade in GDP has been rising steadily. Moreover, most countries in the region have succeeded in raising the value content of their exports by moving into increasingly sophisticated, knowledge-intensive areas of production such as electronics, machine tools, and computing equipment. For most countries in East Asia, success in international trade and the development of more diverse and more sophisticated export structures has been closely related to success in attracting foreign investment. This began in the mid-1980s. But as Figure 14 demonstrates, foreign capital inflows accelerated in the 1990s. In 1997, four countries in East Asia — China, Malaysia, Indonesia, and Thailand — accounted for around 40 per cent of capital flows to developing countries. At the other end of the spectrum, sub-Saharan Africa accounts for less than 1 per cent.[159]

In contrast, Latin America has also attracted huge inflows of private capital in the 1990s. However, a far higher proportion of these inflows have been invested in speculative, rather than productive, activity. Unlike East Asia, Latin America has been spectacularly unsuccessful in channelling foreign investment either into labour-intensive production, or into the transfer of skills and technology.[160]

Growth and employment

Between 1986 and 1993, employment in East Asia increased by more than 3 per cent a year — a figure which was well in excess of the rate of growth in the labour force. Rapid increases in manufacturing output were accompanied by rising real wages, averaging between 3 per cent and 6 per cent a year. The contrast with Latin America is instructive. Between 1991 and 1995, regional growth in Latin America averaged 3 per cent per annum, modest by comparison with the 1970s but double the average rate of the 1980s. Over the same period, the unemployment rate for the region rose, despite the economic recovery. The inverse relationship between growth and employment creation has been a characteristic of most countries, the most extreme case being that of Argentina, where a 3 per cent growth rate has been accompanied by a 7 per cent rise in unemployment.[161]

Earlier, we pointed to the 'poverty-reduction elasticity of growth' as a major feature distinguishing East Asia from other developing regions. East Asian growth has a high elasticity for poverty reduction, in part because the employment elasticity of growth is higher. The latter is an indicator of the relationship between value-added by manufacturing output growth and the creation of employment. For countries such as Mexico, Brazil, India, Pakistan, and the Philippines, each percentage point of manufacturing growth produces less than one-half of the employment creation experienced in countries such as Indonesia and Malaysia. The reason is that the former countries have relied on capital-intensive growth to achieve industrial development. Perversely, employment opportunities have even been restricted by policies penalising labour-intensive industries, such as high import barriers for basic technologies and other imported materials needed to improve productivity. Small-scale industries with an export capacity have been forced to purchase from high-cost local suppliers, while over-valued exchange rates have further compromised their competitiveness. Employment and investment opportunities have been lost as a result.

Another explanation for East Asia's success and Latin America's failure in translating growth into poverty reduction is that, in the latter case, real wages have not increased with output growth. For the region as a whole, real wages were lower in 1995 than in 1981, reflecting the weak linkage to growth. Even where jobs are created in the formal sector, there is no guarantee that wages will be sufficient to reduce poverty. According to one recent report from the Economic Commission for Latin America, a high and growing proportion of the poor in the region are now employed. This reflects the increase in low-waged, often seasonal, employment in agriculture, with women workers in particular suffering a combination of low wages and weak social welfare protection. In Chile, the majority of the poor are in employment.[162] Whereas in East Asia the pattern was one of growth built on rising productivity, with the gains being passed on in the form of rising real wages, in Latin America, the pattern has been one of low-productivity, low-skill employment, with stagnating real wages.[163]

The background to East Asia's success

Not all East Asian countries have followed the same route to develop a manufacturing base capable of sustaining rising real incomes and employment level. Still less, has that successful outcome been the result solely of macro-economic management. Social policies and the extension of educational opportunities have been crucial to economic growth. This book does not attempt to review the wide range of national policies pursued, but once again, some broad trends can be identified.[164] Four of the most important are outlined below.

Selective protection and import substitution

Most countries in the region developed their manufacturing base behind high, but carefully structured, protective barriers. During the 1950s and the first half of the 1960s South Korea developed a labour-intensive manufacturing industry protected by direct import controls. However, trade policy was more liberal for the essential imports needed to increase productivity. After the mid-1960s, government policy combined import protection with export promotion, providing companies with time-bound support in the shape of subsidised credit and preferential access to foreign exchange. In both South Korea and Taiwan, exports surged after the early 1960s, yet the trade regime was a model of controls designed to promote domestic investment.

Less successful as a model of import substitution was Indonesia, where average tariffs in excess of 500 per cent prevailed in the 1970s, shielding domestic companies that were uncompetitive and dominated by vested interests. Not only did the manufacturing sector fail, at this stage, to make a contribution to exports, there is evidence that it slowed overall growth rates and limited employment creation. By the early 1980s, subsidies to loss-making state enterprises accounted for 30 per cent of GDP. In Malaysia, the Proton car has become a symbol of the problems and potential in import substitution. This is the product of a joint venture between the state, domestic investors, and foreign transnational companies. The venture almost collapsed in the 1980s, but by the early 1990s, domestic suppliers were providing 80 per cent of components, and exports began to increase, providing a stimulus to investment and employment.

Regulation of foreign investment

East Asia has been a focal point for direct foreign investment since the mid-1980s. Initially, the impetus came from the 1987 Plaza Accord, which devalued the dollar against the yen and gave Japanese companies an incentive to relocate to production sites with weaker currencies. Even before this, however, Malaysia had combined import protection with generous incentives to foreign investors under its New Economic Policy. These investors concentrated their activities in the electronics sector, where basic assembly operations led the export boom. One of the few requirements was that foreign investors cover the costs of their imports through their export earnings: a measure designed to protect the balance of payments and limit competition for local capital resources. In Indonesia, the surge in direct foreign investment after the early 1980s was accompanied by imports of new technologies which led to a dramatic increase in exports of textiles, clothing, and footwear.

From different policy perspectives, both South Korea and Singapore regulated foreign investment tightly. South Korea prohibited foreign majority-ownership, reserving strategic industrial sectors for domestic investors, who were provided with incentives for building local capacity. In Singapore, foreign investment was encouraged, but channelled into high value-added areas such as fibre optics, banking, and precision technologies. Foreign investors were required to meet targets for training local staff and transferring technologies.

Other countries have been less successful in integrating foreign investment. Under the New Economic Policy, Malaysia provided generous incentives to foreign investors. At one level the results were impressive. The share of manufactured goods in exports rose from 12 per cent to almost 80 per cent between 1970 and 1990, with electronic goods assembled by Malays leading the way. Employment more than doubled and real wages rose at rates in excess of 3 per cent a year. However, Malaysia failed to develop linkages between domestic producers and foreign enterprises, which operated in an import-export enclave. Technology and skills transfer was limited. With Malaysia now facing growing competition from cheaper-labour economies in the region, these policy failures have emerged as a threat to continued prosperity.

Selective liberalisation

Starting with South Korea in the late 1960s, most East Asian countries have moved towards more liberalised systems, often under external pressure. Malaysia's Industrial Master Plan (1986-1995) relaxed the import controls of the New Economic Policy, although import barriers remained high and foreign ownership in domestic industries was limited. In Indonesia, liberalisation started in 1983, but progress in this direction has been limited. Disputes between the Indonesian government and the industrialised countries over the protection afforded to the national car industry underlie the growing tension between industrial policy in the region and international trade rules. In most areas of manufacturing, there has been little liberalisation in the 1990s. It is a similar story in Thailand, although tariffs in most areas remain low by international standards.

As the above account suggests, there are dangers in attempting to draw universal lessons from East Asia. There are also dangers in overstating the region's success. Thailand has been highly ineffective in developing the infrastructure for transport, training, and research and development, which was crucial to the success of South Korea and Taiwan. Failure to upgrade labour skills has reflected the deeper failure of state policy in education discussed earlier. In Malaysia, the economy remains heavily dependent on foreign capital and technology for its manufactured exports. Linkages between the export-oriented transnational company subsidiaries and the rest of the economy remain exceptionally weak. Both countries have suffered from a failure to develop more integrated industrial structures. The same is true of Indonesia, where the bulk of foreign investment is concentrated either in unskilled assembly operations, which create jobs but offer little by way of skills transfer; or in extractive industries such as mining, which create few jobs and wreak environmental havoc, in return for increased foreign exchange earnings.

Reliance on cheap labour as the main source of export growth has also brought with it intra-regional tensions. Wages are higher in countries such as Malaysia, Thailand, and Indonesia than in Vietnam or China, raising the spectre of a massive relocation of capital and employment as the latter countries develop. Some electronics companies have already relocated from Malaysia to Vietnam. So far, however, there is limited evidence of footloose foreign investors shifting the location of production sites. Even in labour-intensive sectors, the costs of establishing operations are relatively high, as are the costs of relocation, serving as a deterrent. But if exaggeration is unwarranted, so too is complacency. Clothes retailers in Europe, for instance, are shifting their sourcing to countries with lower wage levels.

High savings

Another of East Asia's strengths has been its capacity for savings. According to some, this has now emerged as a weakness because of an imbalance between savings and productive investment. Average savings rates in the region are around 30 per cent of national income, compared to under 20 per cent in Latin America. Low-income China saves an extraordinary 40 per cent of national income; middle-income Mexico saves 15 per cent. These high levels of savings have enabled investment to be financed domestically, reducing exposure to the problems of debt and dependence on aid which have characterised Latin America and Africa. A more negative interpretation, most powerfully presented by the Harvard economist Jeffrey Sachs, is that high savings rates are part of East Asia's current problems. This is because, according to this analysis, savings have been directed towards investments which have increased output but failed to increase productivity, which has contributed to a situation in which manufacturing output has been increased to the point where it has lowered prices and profits, creating acute debt problems in the process (as in South Korea). The imbalance between savings and productive investment has also been reflected in the high levels of investment in real estate and financial services, which helped to inflate the speculative bubbles in Thailand and Indonesia to such disastrous effect (see Chapter 7).[165]

Some broad policy lessons

There are no universal blueprints for successful industrial policy to be drawn from East Asia. As in other areas, however, there are some broad lessons of relevance to national and international policy formulation. One lesson is that 'big bang' approaches to liberalisation, in which trade restrictions are withdrawn across-the-board, financial systems deregulated, and foreign investment controls abandoned, are unlikely to succeed. In much of sub-Saharan Africa and Latin America, labour-intensive industries have collapsed under the weight of competition from imports. Trade liberalisation in Latin America has undermined employment in labour-intensive industries without creating new employment opportunities to absorb labour at equivalent income levels. In West Africa, the decline of the textile industry is one example of how trade liberalisation has undermined employment in sectors ill-equipped to adjust to new competitive pressures because of shortages of foreign exchange and capital. Meanwhile, the deregulation of finance and investment can have the effect of concentrating growth in areas, such as financial services, where employment linkages are weak.

The pace and sequencing of reforms is important. So, too, is the composition of employment and production in the sectors subject to liberalisation. The case of Mexico illustrates in extreme form how unbalanced liberalisation and reckless financial deregulation can concentrate the benefits of liberalisation on the rich and the costs on the poor. More generally, trade liberalisation cannot be pursued successfully in the absence of adequate social policies. Countries such as Thailand, Indonesia, and China began a process of liberalisation after they had invested heavily in attempting to raise the skills levels of their work forces. In Latin America, trade liberalisation has been pursued without sufficient attention being paid to policies needed to improve productivity through education and skills training. Trade liberalisation has often cost jobs rather than created opportunities.

Investment policy can play a crucial role in raising skills levels. In South Korea, foreign investment was tightly controlled in the interests of developing indigenous capacity. In Singapore, it was regulated to ensure that skills and technology were transferred. The danger now is that new international rules designed by the industrialised countries in the interests of powerful transnational companies will limit the capacity of governments to regulate foreign investment in the public interest. Under the Multilateral Investment Agreement on Investment (MAI), drawn up by the OECD as the framework for a multilateral agreement, governments will be prevented from establishing controls in areas such as profit repatriation, technology transfer, local-content requirements (under which investors are required to source their operations from local firms), skills training, and balance-of-payments provisions (controls requiring foreign investors to cover the costs of their own imports). These are the very controls which have enabled East Asian countries to use foreign investment successfully for the creation of long-term growth and employment. Surrendering sovereignty in this area carries the threat of allowing anarchic-capitalism to flourish, when governments would effectively lose the capacity to regulate economic life in the interests of their citizens.

Export opportunity is an often neglected component of the East Asian success story. The first generation of 'tiger' economies emerged during a period in which world trade was expanding and becoming increasingly open. Today, many of the poorest countries face a bewildering array of tariff barriers. Under the Uruguay Round these barriers were reduced, but by considerably less for developing countries than for developed countries. In areas such as textiles, leather, oilseeds, and other agricultural goods, import barriers remain a powerful deterrent to diversification. Removing that deterrent would do much to enable poor countries to trade their way into recovery.

International action is also needed to remove the millstone of foreign debt, which has been happily absent from the collective necks of the East Asian countries. The burden is most serious in sub-Saharan Africa. If South Africa is excluded, the region's debt-to-export ratio is 327 per cent, compared to a World Bank sustainability ceiling of 200-250 per cent.[166] High levels of debt overhang, which this figure reflects, act as a major deterrent to investment. Meanwhile, debt servicing (amounting to around $10bn annually) has the effect of reducing the foreign exchange available for essential imports, hampering the competitiveness of local industries. The Highly Indebted Poor Countries (HIPC) debt initiative could act as a spur to growth by reducing debt overhang and increasing import capacity. However, it provides insufficient debt relief over an unacceptably long time-frame. A further problem is the requirement that potentially eligible countries comply with IMF stabilisation programmes, which have a poor track record in restoring growth and investment.

5 Rural development through redistribution

Investment in human development was a precondition for East Asia's rapid industrialisation, and the transition to more sophisticated areas of production. Here we discuss the third foundation for East Asia's success: the redistribution of productive assets and the creation of opportunities in rural areas. Policies in this area enabled poor people to participate in growth as producers and investors, rather than as passive beneficiaries of income transfers from the top down. Allied to other pro-poor policies, redistribution helped to unleash the productive potential of poor people and to spread the benefits of growth more widely, demonstrating again that poverty reduction can be a cause as well as an outcome of faster growth.

The success of East Asian countries in reducing rural poverty was achieved partly through developments beyond the agricultural sector, through the availability of industrial employment for rural-urban migrants. But policies within the rural sector have also been important. Most importantly, rural development and poverty reduction have been built on policies and programmes which support smallholder agriculture. In varying ways, Korea, Taiwan, Indonesia, Malaysia and, more recently, China and Vietnam have all followed this strategy. Each of these countries broke up large-scale holdings and encouraged their development into smallholder systems.[167] As a result, the share of crops grown by smallholders increased. Redistributive land reform was part of a wider strategy. Each of the East Asian countries also invested heavily in agricultural infrastructure and technology for smallholders. Specific interventions have included investment in marketing infrastructure and services, the creation of rural credit and savings facilities, protection against cheap imports, and price stabilisation.

This strategy of support for smallholders has not sacrificed efficiency for equity. Evidence from a number of countries confirms the superior productivity of smallholder agriculture.[168] It also points to stronger linkages between smallholder production on the one side, and employment creation and poverty reduction on the other. The dramatic decline in rural poverty in East Asia makes the region a compelling model for others to follow. This is especially true of countries where highly concentrated land structures sacrifice both efficiency and equity to the power of vested interests.[169]

The majority of poor people in developing countries (well over half, outside of Latin America) depend on agriculture for their livelihoods. In Latin America, the rural poor are a minority, but their poverty is far deeper than that of the urban poor. In all developing regions, inadequate access to land is one of the primary causes of rural poverty. According to the Food and Agricultural Organisation of the UN, over one-third of smallholders in sub-Saharan Africa and Asia subsist on plots too small to support their families. Another 180 million people worldwide are landless, and among the poorest of the poor.

Access to land is one of the most basic requirements for participation in growth. Another is access to markets. Poverty is often concentrated in areas where inadequate access to rural feeder roads, and poor storage facilities, restrict rural incomes. In most cases, investment in marketing infrastructure is concentrated around commercial (usually irrigated) farm areas, while more marginal (usually rain-fed) areas are neglected. The same applies to public investment in agricultural research. Staple food-crops such as sorghum, millet, beans, and cassava, which are grown and consumed by poor people, are given a low priority. This is reflected in the slow rate of increase in production and yields, and is an important factor behind rural poverty. Access to capital can act as another constraint. Institutional finance is unavailable to around 80 per cent of rural households in developing countries. Women farmers have the least access of all. In Africa, women farmers account for almost two-thirds of the agricultural labour force and 80 per cent of food production, yet they receive only 1 per cent of the credit provided to agriculture.[170] To the structural problems can be added wider policy problems. For instance, prices are often biased against agriculture, with over-valued exchange rates reducing the price for competitive food imports and depressing the local currency value of exports.

The failure of governments to remove the multiple constraints on the productivity of the rural poor is rooted partly in an unwillingness to challenge powerful vested interests and risk political instability; and partly in a conviction that smallholder agriculture is less efficient than large-scale-commercial agriculture. Evidence from East Asia suggests that the risk assessment is flawed, and that the efficiency assessment in comprehensively wrong.

Five myths about big farms

Policies promoting smallholder agriculture as outlined above have a good record in facilitating poverty reduction and improving equity. But have gains in these areas been achieved at the expense of growth? If not, what are the obstacles to policy action? The case against redistributive reforms in favour of smallholder agriculture is sustained by five myths:

• *Myth 1:* 'The poor are inefficient users of scarce land and capital resources.' In fact, international evidence suggests that when land quality is taken into account, there is an inverse relationship between the size of plot and productivity. That relationship becomes more pronounced for farms larger than 30 acres. In general, small farmers invest more intensively in farm improvements such as wells and terracing.[171]

• *Myth 2:* 'Small farms do not create employment or reduce poverty.' In fact, small farms employ more people per hectare than large farms. Growth of output on these farms therefore tends to generate more employment per acre. Smallholder farming also spreads the value of production more widely. For politicians genuinely concerned to expand agricultural productivity, increase rural employment, and promote poverty reduction, smallholder agriculture is the most efficient route.[172]

• *Myth 3:* 'Big farms are efficient and create jobs.' Big farms tend to produce bigger surpluses for domestic and foreign markets, which is not the same thing. Large-scale farms typically enjoy subsidised access to scarce foreign-exchange and capital resources, for investing in imported chemicals and capital equipment. The subsidies are rarely taken into account when measuring efficiency. Nor are the costs in terms of lost output and employment resulting from the diversion of foreign exchange from smallholder agriculture and labour-intensive manufacturing. Capital-intensive production means that employment creation has been weak on large farms, helping to explain the failure to translate agricultural growth into poverty reduction.

• *Myth 4:* 'Land reform will disrupt production.' There has been too little genuine land reform to test this assertion. However, what evidence there is points in the other direction. Land reform in Japan, South Korea, and Taiwan was followed by significant gains in productivity. The same is true of the land-reform programmes introduced in Kerala during the 1970s and West Bengal in the 1980s.[173]

• *Myth 5:* 'Land redistribution creates political instability.' So does the absence of land reform. The desperation of the rural poor in Brazil is revealed by increasingly frequent land invasions to occupy under-utilised land on large holdings.[174] Violence against squatters is intensive. In Zimbabwe, the independence war was fought for land, and the failure of government to introduce land reform is a source of political resentment and social tension.

Land reform as an engine of growth

Radical land redistribution, the elimination of absentee land ownership, resettlement, and the imposition of land ceilings have acted as powerful forces for empowerment and the creation of opportunities for the rural poor across much of East Asia. In the 1950s, South Korea and Taiwan followed Japan in introducing reforms which displaced landlords, set limits on land ownership, and gave tenants a stake in the land. From 1960 to 1970, hundreds of thousands of smallholders were resettled on large-scale plantations in Malaysia and given titles to individual plots. The result was a marked reduction in the inequality of land holding. Indonesia started out with a more equal distribution of land, but it too embarked on a major resettlement programme over the same period, with plantations being broken up and parcelled out to smallholders. From a different political direction, China and Vietnam broke the power of landlords by collectivising land-holdings. The end result of these reforms is that East Asia has the world's most equal system of land ownership. The Gini coefficient for land distribution (as for income, this moves from 0 [perfect equality] towards 1 as inequality increases) is 0.33, compared to 0.70 for Latin America.[175] Land redistribution enabled poor rural households to impart a new dynamic to the growth process. It also created a form of social protection. China's highly egalitarian system of land ownership has been a causal factor in the absence of hunger and malnutrition on the scale witnessed in most other low-income countries. Access to land has meant that poor households have been able to meet their calorie needs. Thus, although rural income inequalities widened in the 1980s, malnutrition did not increase. In effect, access to land has enabled households to provide their own social protection, reducing dependence on transfers in cash or in kind from the state. In any country with a weak administrative infrastructure and limited resources available for government intervention, this is a far more effective strategy for reducing the risk of malnutrition than reliance on state institutions.

'Getting the prices right' by removing distortions against the poor was part of the success story in China, but only one part. Until the late 1970s, farmers in China were required to work collectively and deliver their surpluses to the government. In effect, they were government employees receiving a wage dictated by the state. Private initiative was stifled and production stagnated. The situation changed dramatically with the introduction of the 'household's responsibility' system, under which households assumed responsibility for individual plots. Marketing remained in the hands of the state, but households were allowed to sell their produce separately and retain the income. This provided peasants with greater incentives to increase output and productivity. Agricultural growth accelerated to over 7 per cent a year in the six years after 1978, double the average for the previous ten years.[176] Meanwhile, the incidence of rural poverty, measured against the national minimum food consumption poverty line, fell from 28 per cent to less than 10 per cent as rural incomes doubled over the same period. Good access to land and productive inputs, the highly developed marketing infrastructure, and a well-financed programme of agricultural research meant that poor people were in a position to respond to — and benefit from — market opportunities.

The same picture emerges from Vietnam, where rural producers participated in a collective system of labour which limited incentives. By the mid-1980s, the rural economy was in crisis and food self-sufficiency in steep decline. As in China, rural communities were locked into a situation of egalitarian stagnation. This changed in 1986 when Vietnam followed the Chinese example. Under *doi moi*, government retained a quasi-monopolistic position in the marketing of rice, but individual households were given responsibility for their own piece of land; in effect, decollectivising their labour.[177] The results were astonishing. Within six years Vietnam was the world's second largest exporter of rice after Thailand and the US, with agricultural output rising at rates of over 6 per cent a year. In both cases, there was a high level of participation in the expansion of the rural economy with the benefits widely, if unequally, shared.

Success and failure in agrarian reform

There are many examples of land reform failing because of poor design and inadequate attention to supportive measures, such as the development of marketing infrastructure. The land-reform programme in Mexico in the 1930s was the most equitable to date, but it failed to empower peasants economically because associated development measures were weak. The same was true of the limited land-resettlement programme introduced after independence in Zimbabwe. In the Philippines, legislation for a Comprehensive Agrarian Reform Programme (CARP) was passed ten years ago. Its express purpose was to enhance smallholder access to land, an imperative for poverty reduction in the Philippines, where 36 per cent of land was controlled by 2 per cent of producers.[178] Yet ten years on, the programme remains uncompleted.

But if failure has characterised many efforts at land reform, there are some success stories to confirm the lessons from East Asia. For example, in West Bengal, the implementation of land-ceiling laws resulted in land transfers to 1.4 million people. Another 2.1 million tenants benefited from Operation Barga, a legislative programme launched in 1978 to fix the share of the crop that could be claimed by landlords, provide security of tenure, and end arbitrary evictions. In total, around half of all households in West Bengal benefited from the reforms, over 40 per cent of the total number of beneficiaries in India. Effects on production have been positive. Before land reform, growth in production in West Bengal was some 30 per cent lower than the national average, and well below the rate of increase in population.[179] During the 1980s food grain output rose at 3.4 per cent, compared to a 2.7 per cent national average. Human development indicators also improved. Central to the success of West Bengal's programme was popular participation in the implementation of reforms. Village *panchayats* (councils), provided a political base for the state government, registering claims and titles and defending the rights of beneficiaries. As such they played a central role in redistributing power from landed elites to an alliance of small farmers and the landless poor, creating the political conditions in which land reform could succeed.

In situations of extreme land inequality and high levels of rural poverty, there is no alternative to land redistribution as a first step towards poverty reduction. The case of Zimbabwe, where inequality in land ownership has excluded the rural poor from opportunities to participate in markets, graphically illustrates the problem. While it is an extreme case, it has similarities with Kenya and neighbouring countries, where land ownership is becoming more concentrated. It is also not untypical of the type of land-ownership patterns found in Latin America, where agrarian reform has been long delayed but remains an imperative for poverty reduction.

Excluding the poor: land-holding in Zimbabwe

Zimbabwe represents in extreme form the efficiency and equity problems associated with large-scale agriculture.[180] At independence the country inherited one of the world's most unequal land systems. Little has changed since. Some 4,400 mainly white-owned commercial farms and ranches occupy one-third of the country's arable land, and over 80 per cent of the prime-quality land located in areas of high rainfall. Drive west from Harare and the route passes through some of the richest farmland in Africa. Vast estates averaging 2,200 hectares in size produce vegetables and flowers for Europe and maize for the domestic market. Continue on the same route and you reach Masvingo, an overcrowded and ecologically degraded farming area in which over half of house-holds live in poverty. Most farms are less than one hectare in size — insufficient to produce enough food for more than four months. Soil erosion has reached chronic proportions, limiting productivity and forcing households to transfer labour to towns and commercial farming areas.

Inequality in land ownership is at the heart of the poverty problem facing Zimbabwe. The country has one of the highest Gini coefficients in the world for income distribution, limiting the benefits which growth creates for poor people. At the same time, skewed land ownership prevents poor rural producers from contributing to growth and is a source of inefficiency. Less than 15 per cent of commercial farm land is under cultivation, with farmers producing only on their most profitable fields.[181] Minimal taxes on commercial farm land make it possible to leave the rest idle, in effect wasting one of the country's prime assets.

Places like Masvingo are typical of the communal farming areas in which over 6 million black smallholder farmers eke out an existence on poor-quality soils. Local initiatives are attempting to develop more secure livelihood structures. Oxfam works in Masvingo with partners who are supporting the efforts of women farmers by providing small amounts of credit, developing water-harvesting techniques, and sup-porting market-gardening initiatives, enabling households to grow vegetables for sale or home consumption. These initiatives are aimed at creating additional income, diversifying food supplies, and providing productive employment. Except in drought years, they help to reduce vulnerability and improve nutrition. Ultimately, however, local-level initiatives cannot provide a framework for poverty reduction in the absence of redistributive land-reform measures. There are 2.5 million people in rural Zimbabwe who are too poor to meet their basic needs.[182] Malnutrition among children is high, reaching up to 30 per cent in many districts.[183] Some of the most appalling sights of human deprivation are to be found on the commercial farms, where labourers pick fruit and vegetables for export to Europe, but are unable to feed themselves. Without a fundamental shift in land ownership patterns, it is unlikely that the rural poor will be able to lift themselves out of poverty.

Zimbabwe's land system helps to explain why, despite the country's achievements in social policy, it has been unable to establish a foundation for growth with equity on the Vietnamese path. Under its economic reform programme with the IMF-World Bank, the Zimbabwean government is relying on market incentives to improve the position of the rural poor. Since the vast majority of the rural poor are excluded from effective participation in markets because of the limited size and poor quality of their holdings, the prospects of success are limited. As one World Bank assessment puts it: 'Even under the most favourable scenario, it would be expected that only 15 to 20 per cent of smallholder households would participate directly in the expansion of agricultural production.'[184] The scenario in question did not include the option of land redistribution.

The power of vested interests: the failure of land reform in Brazil

If the case for land reform is so strong in social and economic terms, why is it so unwillingly embraced by governments? Largely because of the power of vested interests. In Brazil, for example, less than two per cent of landholders own over 80 per cent of cultivable land. The largest 35,000 landowners own an area equal in size to Germany, France, Spain and Austria, with Switzerland thrown in for good measure. At the other end of the rural hierarchy are up to 4 million landless, or near-landless, rural households. Many were uprooted to make way for large commercial estates in the 1970s, when Brazil emerged as a major power in agricultural export markets. The country is now one of the largest suppliers of high-protein animal feedstuffs to Europe. Meanwhile, impoverished rural households are unable to feed themselves, their nutritional needs occupying a lower priority in national policy than the nutritional needs of European cows.

Since the mid-1980s, popular demands for land reform have been growing in force. The Movimento do Trabalhadores (MST) has emerged as a major force, supporting occupation as the first step towards social justice and a more rational land system. Political support for the MST has been growing, in part as a consequence of recognition that Brazil's land system is grossly inefficient as well as grossly unjust. Only 14 per cent of the commercial farm-land is under cultivation, wasting one of the country's prime assets. In principle the government now recognises the strength of the MST's demands, but is moving slowly — offering to settle up to 200,000 people by the end of the decade instead of supporting a radical programme of land redistribution. Its hesitation is rooted not in economic logic, but in the power of national and provincial elites and vested interests.

Building an enabling environment

Land redistribution is a potential first step towards poverty reduction and improved efficiency. It is not a stand-alone strategy. To varying degrees, governments in East Asia have attempted to support rural livelihoods and promote productivity through a mixture of price incentives and infrastructural support. An important objective in most cases has been the attainment of national self-sufficiency through smallholder producers, with national food systems protected against competition from imports.

The case of Indonesia is instructive. In the decade from the mid-1970s to the mid-1980s the country went from being the world's largest food-deficit country, importing over 2 million tons of rice annually, to being self-sufficient.[185] Public investment in irrigation, the promotion of heavy-yielding varieties of rice, and a phenomenal increase in the use of artificial fertilisers were central to this achievement. So, too, was price stabilisation. The government marketing agency, the Bulog, operated a food reserve which enabled it to keep prices above a floor and below a ceiling. It was also given sole authority to import grains, ensuring that cheap imports did not drive down local prices below the agreed floor. This reduced the risks of investment, and raised returns to smallholder rice farmers, helping to accelerate the move towards self-sufficiency.[186]

Not all governments in the region have succeeded in protecting rural producers against fluctuations in world prices. In Thailand, the government was less effective during the 1980s in providing price support, with damaging consequences for rural poverty. In the mid-1980s, subsidised over-production and export dumping by the United States and the European Union reduced world prices for food grains to their lowest levels since the 1930s. Rice was one of the commodities affected, with the US using its Export Enhancement Programme to expand market shares. In Indonesia, the Bulog protected producers from the price slump by effectively banning imports. In Thailand, authorities allowed domestic prices to fall to international levels. Rural poverty increased sharply in Thailand, especially in the poor rice-producing areas of the north-east, while it continued to decline in Indonesia.[187] Meanwhile, productivity gains began to slow in Thailand during the second half of the 1980s as a result of declining investment.

Contrasts between countries in East Asia and the rest of the developing world are marked. In much of sub-Saharan Africa and Latin America, governments have systematically encouraged cheap food imports as a means of reducing food prices for urban populations. While Indonesia was using its oil revenues in the 1980s to invest in the productive potential of its food producers, Nigeria went in the other direction, using oil revenues to finance food imports. Between 1975 and 1985 it made the transition from being self-sufficient in basic staples to being sub-Saharan Africa's largest food importer.[188]

The rest of sub-Saharan Africa followed a similar pattern. Production of local food staples such as cassava and millet fell by an average of 1 per cent per capita over the two decades up to 1990. Competition from cheap, usually subsidised, imports has been an important factor reducing incentives to producers in many countries. Dependence on the same imports has increased at an alarming rate.[189] Today, sub-Saharan Africa spends around one-third of its foreign exchange earnings on imported foodstuffs. This represents a huge diversion of import capacity in a sector where, with adequate support, smallholder farmers could achieve national food self-reliance. It also leaves the region in a precarious food-security situation, with foreign debt and trade problems jeopardising the capacity to maintain imports.

The threat of food dumping

The evidence from East Asia suggests that protection against subsidised food dumping is crucial to the development of rural prosperity and poverty reduction. However, international trade arrangements have emerged as a potential obstacle to effective action. In Mexico, the national maize market is being liberalised under the North American Free Trade Agreement, a move which will bring domestic maize producers into direct competition with (subsidised) farmers in the US Mid-West. Since most Mexican peasant farmers grow corn on poor rain-fed land with low yields (one-quarter of the US average) and little investment in inputs, corn imports from the US will undermine local producers. According to one study, over 2 million livelihoods could be lost as a result, most of them in rain-fed areas where the highest incidence of poverty is to be found.[190]

From a different direction, similar threats face some of the poorest producers in the Philippines. Under the Uruguay Round world trade agreement, the Philippines has committed itself to removing import quotas for corn and replacing them with tariffs, which will be reduced by half between now and 2004. Projections suggest that cheaper imports from the US and Thailand will lower the household incomes of corn-producing households by 15–30 per cent. The social costs could be high. Around 1.2 million households in the Philippines, concentrated in Mindanao and the Cagayan Valley, depend on income from corn sales for their livelihoods. It has been estimated that around one-quarter of these households could lose their livelihoods as a direct consequence of market liberalisation.[191] The social costs will be enormous. Around half of corn producing households live below the poverty line. Infant mortality rates in both of the main producing regions are among the highest in the country. Apart from the direct effects on corn-producing households, the wider rural economy will suffer as falling incomes translate into reduced demand for locally-produced goods.

Mexico and the Philippines illustrate wider problems associated with liberalisation in markets characterised by high levels of rural poverty. Weak competitiveness in the smallholder sectors of both countries is partly a consequence of inadequate support to smallholders. In the Philippines, public spending on rural infrastructure is lower as a share of GDP than in any other Asian country. Over half of the country's *barangays* lack all-weather roads, raising the costs of marketing. Roads are particularly poorly developed in the corn-producing regions of Mindanao, which is one of the reasons for the low competitiveness of domestic produce against imports.

In both countries, trade liberalisation is seen by governments as part of a wider strategy to boost economic growth by forcing domestic food producers to compete against imports, while expanding agricultural exports. From a distributional perspective, the problem with this approach is that the winners from export opportunities are not necessarily the same as the losers from import liberalisation. In Mexico, the growth point for the export-oriented part of the rural economy is located in the irrigated districts of the North Pacific Coast, the valleys of El Bajo, and the coastline along the Gulf of Mexico. Production is dominated by a few thousand large commercial farms exporting fruit and vegetables to the US. Meanwhile, the smallholder sector is collapsing under the weight of government neglect and competition from imports. In terms of land use, the fruit and vegetable sector accounts for about 6 per cent of cultivated area, but 40 per cent of the value of exports; the maize sector accounts for half of cultivated land, the majority of peasant livelihoods, and only 20 per cent of output.[192] Rain-fed smallholder areas, where the majority of losers will be found, will inevitably be subject to out-migration, with a growing number of women joining a rural labour force employed on a casual basis on commercial farm estates. The overall effect will be to widen the gap between rich and poor producers, and between the 'misery belt' in the South and wealthier states linked to the US economy in the North.

'Protectionism' in agriculture is not an inherently pro-poor strategy. In Nigeria, large-scale commercial wheat farmers have absorbed huge subsidies, with a few producers benefiting at the expense of the many. By contrast, because the vast majority of rice farmers in Indonesia are smallholders, infrastructural investment, extension services, and price support had positive distributional effects, while at the same time helping to underpin the attainment of food self-sufficiency. Another strength of price support in Indonesia was the fact that domestic prices were maintained at levels which were not wildly out of line with (unsubsidised) world market prices, limiting costs and acting as a check on efficiency.

Whatever the broad case for and against protectionism, the case for liberalisation in world markets as they presently operate is weak. These markets are dominated by the OECD countries, which collectively spend around $180bn annually on agricultural subsidies, including export subsidies, which represents around 40 per cent of the total value of their farm output.[193] The US, the world's largest exporter and a 'crusader' for free trade in agricultural matters, spends in excess of $16bn annually in subsidising production and exports. The EU spends considerably more. Faced with competition on this scale from the treasuries of the world's wealthiest countries, smallholder farmers in the developing world will inevitably suffer lost livelihood opportunities and lower incomes.

Institutional credit

Along with agrarian reform and appropriate pricing policies, access to credit is another part of the integrated strategy for growth, equity, and poverty reduction. Research has consistently shown that poor producers are a good risk and are able to secure high returns on limited investment. Repayment rates for small-scale credit schemes in excess of 90 per cent are not uncommon — and they are not matched by a comparable repayment performance on the part of subsidised credit agencies serving large-scale producers. From a broader livelihoods perspective, credit services can provide assistance in times of crisis, averting the need for households to engage in distress sales of assets, and provide the investment resources that enable people to seize market opportunities. In Vietnam, the number of borrowers from the Vietnam Bank of

Agriculture increased seven-fold in the first half of the 1990s, to over seven million people, as rural producers responded to the opportunities created by market reforms.[194] Credit, however, is only one part of the equation. The poor can also save, and their savings can provide the resources needed to develop credit facilities at a local level. Where available, savings services enable people to store wealth as an insurance strategy, to accumulate funds for future investment in areas such as education and production, and to secure a return on their assets.

Effective credit and savings institutions providing micro-finance services can enhance the position of the poor by providing a secure haven for savings, with interest payments preventing their erosion through inflation; and by decreasing risks and facilitating productive investment.[195] In the absence of credible financial institutions, poor people develop their own informal savings and credit arrangements. There are an infinite variety of informal 'self-help' saving schemes operating in communities across the developing world, and an equally infinite variety of informal lending schemes. In some cases, especially where creditors enjoy a monopolistic position, the latter can be highly exploitative. Non-government agencies have become extensively involved in credit provision. Perhaps the best known example is that of the Grameen Bank in Bangladesh, which provides credit to 2 million people, most of them women who would otherwise be excluded. At the other end of the scale are a wide range of small-scale initiatives. In the Eastern Province of Zambia, Oxfam works with women farm co-operatives of between ten and fourteen members, supporting revolving credit funds. This is an area in which four out of every five households live in poverty, and where formal credit is largely absent. The revolving credit funds have enabled women farmers to borrow at subsidised interest rates to purchase seeds, tools and other necessities. Repayment rates have been high, suggesting that the credit has been turned into productive investment.

In Mexico, another of Oxfam's partners, the Regional Union of Support to Farmers (URAC), has developed an integrated savings and credit system servicing 5000 members.[196] Its interest rates are broadly linked to those in the wider market, but it provides services which small producers are unable to get from commercial banks, whose transaction costs and charges are prohibitive for small savers. Because URAC — like the Bank Ralcycat Indonesia (BRI) — mobilises local savings, it is less dependent on support from external donors or borrowing in local markets to finance loans. Only savers are entitled to borrow, creating a sense of ownership. Recent research by Oxfam has shown the important role played by URAC in enabling its members to survive in hard times (for instance, in the event of seasonal unemployment or sickness), to meet the cost of school and health fees, and to finance investment.

But despite the many success stories and a wildly exaggerated press, micro-finance projects have their limits. Targeting the poor is administratively difficult and costly. In some cases the intended beneficiaries become 'carriers' for non-target groups. This is a problem for the Grameen Bank, where recent research has shown women borrowers assuming repayment responsibility for funds transferred to men.[197] Ultimately, however the real problem with micro-credit projects is that they will always be insufficient to meet the needs of the poor. Many schemes are unsustainable, in that they are heavily dependent on external funding and what amount to interest-rate subsidies which, if extended, would render them unaffordable. What are needed are financial institutions which, operating in local and national markets, can mobilise local savings and provide credit through arrangements adapted to meet the needs of the poor.

Indonesia provides an example of one such institution in the shape of the Bank Rakyat Indonesia (BRI), a state-owned commercial bank which began to develop operations in rural areas during the 1970s.[198] Until the mid-1980s, the BRI suffered from many of the same problems as rural banks in other developing countries. Little attention was paid to the mobilisation of savings, which restricted the funds available for lending. Most loans went to local elites, who were considered low risk, while the vast majority of the rural poor borrowed on informal markets at far higher interest rates. Arrears and losses were high, bringing the BRI to the verge of collapse by the early 1980s.

From 1983, the BRI's management initiated a radical change of direction, with the focus shifting from credit delivery to financial intermediation. New savings programmes were developed to provide services to small savers who required a combination of security and easy access. In 1984, rural savers with the BRI were numbered in tens of thousands, with deposits amounting to less than $0.2m. Today, the institution has 13 million deposit accounts holding $2.4bn. Over half of these savers have deposit accounts of less than $12, underlining the success of the BRI in providing services relevant to the poor. By successfully tapping these rural savings, the BRI has been able to increase its lending operations, although loans account for less than one-fifth of savings deposits — a fact which underlines the importance of savings outlets for the poor. Interest rates are far lower than those charged on informal markets but linked to market rates. Once again, most loans to individuals are small and for short terms of 10–12 weeks. Over one-third of the BRI's borrowers have incomes below the poverty lines. In addition to individual loans, the BRI also capitalises 5000 village-level banks. The success of BRI is clear proof of the fact that market-based credit and savings institutions can work as agencies for growth and poverty reduction, mobilising the savings of the poor for investment by the poor.

Some policy lessons

The most important rural development lesson from East Asia is that, given an opportunity, smallholder farmers can produce their way out of poverty and feed their fellow-citizens. Opportunity is the operative word. Access to land, investment in infrastructure, access to credit and savings institutions, and protection from unfair competition are all elements in the range of smallholder strategies developed in East Asia. These strategies have shared in common a concern to build on the initiative and potential of peasant farmers. Positive policy lessons emerge for other countries:

Improve efficiency and equity through land redistribution
Highly unequal land systems are economically inefficient and socially disruptive. Support for land redistribution as an element of a wider agrarian reform strategy should be made central to poverty reduction initiatives.

Create savings and credit institutions for the poor
Poor producers can save, and they are highly efficient investors. Most, however, are denied access to savings and credit agencies, with resultant losses in terms of efficiency and equity. Financial institutions which are accessible to the poor, and deal in small amounts at low transaction costs, are essential.

Provide transport and marketing infrastructure
Because poor producers are often located in marginal areas poorly served by roads, they face difficulties in gaining access to markets and inputs. They are disadvantaged through the lower prices for their output which accompany higher transport costs, while the rest of society loses through lower levels of output.

Respond to needs and build on local knowledge
The Green Revolution brought major productivity and income gains for producers of rice, wheat, and maize. Millions of smallholders benefited.

By contrast, yields for crops such as sorghum, millet, and cassava, produced by the majority of the poor in Africa, have stagnated. New innovations are needed which focus on crops produced by the poor. These innovations should build on indigenous systems of cultivation and focus on previously neglected areas such as tree crops, inter-cropping, pastoral agriculture, and communal agro-forestry.

Some have drawn different conclusions from East Asia's experience. For instance, the World Bank cites it as 'proof' of the need to privatise and individualise land holding. It claims that this is the only way to increase productivity and generate higher levels of credit through the use of land as collateral. However, the argument is flawed. Private land titles are not a pre-condition for rural credit or for raising productivity: neither China nor Vietnam have private land titles. Where private land titles are introduced, they carry the risk of marginalising poor communities whose land rights are rooted in communal, tribal, or ancestral rights, which are often difficult to enforce. In Zambia, Oxfam works with communities who became landless as a consequence of land privatisa-tion, with the state selling their plots to commercial interests. The more sensible option, followed in Tanzania, is to recognise a variety of land rights and to focus on providing security in occupancy.

Another 'lesson' wrongly derived from East Asia is that trade liber-alisation is vital to rural development. For staple food producers, protection from subsidised competition is needed to create investment, production, and employment opportunities. To this end, the World Trade Organisation should adopt a food security clause allowing countries to protect their domestic food systems up to the point of national self-sufficiency. The industrialised countries could further improve matters by agreeing to a comprehensive ban on the dumping of agricultural exports.

6 The limits to growth with equity

Much of this book so far has focused on the positive lessons to emerge from East Asia. But not all the lessons are positive — and some are decidedly negative. While the region may, with significant exceptions, have achieved a high degree of equity in comparison to other developing regions, there have been limits to equity. Behind the tower blocks, expensive hotels, and fashion boutiques which have sprung up in the financial centres of Bangkok, Manila, and Jakarta, nestle slums which would not be out of place in Bolivia or Ethiopia. In the Central Highlands and Northern Uplands of Vietnam, Oxfam works with tribal communities who are being bypassed by the benefits of growth and left increasingly further behind the rest of the country in human development terms. In Cambodia and the Philippines, Oxfam's partners work with indigenous people who are being displaced by domestic and foreign investors granted concessions over their ancestral lands. In China, economic reforms have created new opportunities, along with new social pressures. Income inequalities are growing, progress in human development is slowing, and the rural-urban divide is widening, as is the human welfare gap between coastal and interior provinces.

Across East Asia, rapid growth and urbanisation have been accompanied by social marginalisation. While the 'wealth gap' in most countries may not be wide by international standards, there is a pervasive sense of a 'social justice gap'. That gap is revealed in the violence experienced by poor people in the name of development, and in the widening social differences between rich and poor. The displacement of small farmers to make way for development projects, the violation of the land rights of indigenous groups and ethnic minorities in the interests of powerful domestic and foreign investors, and violent relocations of urban squatter settlements have been part and parcel of the drive for growth.

Natural resource mismanagement has been of epic proportions. Forests have been denuded in the interests of maximising short-term foreign-exchange gains, without regard either to the human costs or to the interests of long-term growth. Communities have suffered at various levels. Forced displacement, and the loss of land and access to communal resources in forests are among the more immediate costs associated with the ruthless prioritisation of growth over human needs. Less immediately apparent are the wider costs associated with environmental destruction. Soil erosion, the siltation of waterways, and the destruction of coastal resources are all consequences of natural resource mismanagement. Had the economic costs in terms of reduced productivity and output of forestry destruction been computed into Indonesia's national accounts in the 1970s, growth rates would have been 2–3 per cent lower. The social costs are less amenable to national accounting devices.

One of the tragedies of East Asia's experience is the failure of governments to learn from past mistakes. In fact, these mistakes are now being exported within the region, notably by Malaysian logging companies entering Cambodia. This reflects a wider failure to develop more participatory and accountable political structures. The poor have little voice and little access to justice, leaving them at the mercy of political structures in which corruption, vested interests, and the subordination of public finances to the accumulation of private wealth flourish.

From Oxfam's perspective, development means more than economic growth and material welfare. It also implies wider citizenship rights, including the right of people to have a say over their future and over the formulation of policies which affect their lives. Such rights are denied on a massive scale in East Asia; and in the absence of moves towards full civil and political rights, future human development and economic growth will be jeopardised. The following section outlines some of the development failures in the region.

Regional inequalities

A common feature of growth in East Asia has been its concentration around urban industrial areas and more commercial agricultural areas. Rural-urban differences are becoming more pronounced, and communities living in geographically isolated areas are being left further behind. During the 1990s, Vietnam has experienced average annual growth rates averaging 6–7 per cent. However, one-third of aggregate economic growth has occurred in Ho Chi Minh city alone. At a provincial level, 14 out of 53 provinces, containing almost one-fifth of the population, experienced a decline in per capita income. The health, education and income gap between these provinces and the lowland delta areas is widening rapidly, with minority groups in particular being left behind. Income poverty incidence ranges from a low of 33 per cent in the southeast to 77 per cent in the north-central region.

In Thailand, rapid economic growth has been centered almost entirely on Bangkok. In no other country of comparable size is manufacturing industry and the locus of growth so heavily centralised. Average per capita incomes in Bangkok are now twice the national average and 15 times the level in the north-east of the country, where poverty is most concentrated. While the benefits of growth have been overwhelmingly urban, the majority of the population — and an even bigger majority of the poor — are rural. This explains why the share of national income accruing to the richest 10 per cent of Thai society has risen from a multiple of 17 times to 38 times that of the poorest 10 per cent since 1981. The north-east has the highest incidence of poverty and accounts for over half of the total number of poor.

As in Thailand, aggregate poverty has fallen dramatically in Indonesia since the 1960s; and, as in Thailand, progress has been uneven. The most impressive gains have been concentrated in and around Jakarta, where income poverty affects just over 1 per cent of the population. In East Nusa Tenggara, 50 per cent of people live below the poverty line.

The image of China as a burgeoning industrial superpower is partially accurate. But it is an image based on Shanghai and the coastal provinces of Jiangsu, Zhejiang, Shandong, and Guangdong, which account for two-thirds of industrial output and over 95 per cent of the foreign investment flooding into the country. Disparities in investment and trade have had powerful effects on income distribution. Since the start of the economic reform process, provincial income disparities have been increasing at an accelerating rate, with average incomes in coastal areas rising at over 2.5 per cent per annum faster than in inland provinces in the 1980s, rising to 5 per cent in the 1990s. As a result, incomes in coastal areas are now around 50 per cent higher than in inland areas. Decentralisation of the fiscal system has exacerbated differences in human welfare performance since richer provinces are able to spend more on health, education, and welfare than poorer ones.

Poverty is becoming increasingly concentrated in remote mountainous and interior regions of the north, north-west, and south-west. In Tibet, the illiteracy rate is 44 per cent — three times the national average. As in Vietnam, minority groups are facing particularly serious forms of marginalisation. Yunnan province in the south is home to 3 per cent of China's population and 10 per cent of those living in poverty. Of this group, around three-quarters are from minorities.

East Asian governments have failed to resolve the problem of spreading opportunities more widely to marginalised areas. Regional planning, redistributive public spending policies to favour poorer regions, increased investment in health, education and marketing infrastructure, and incentives for investors to create employment opportunities away from current growth zones, are some possible approaches. In the extreme case of Thailand, failure to promote a wider dispersion of manufacturing activity and to develop transport and production infrastructures has emerged as a major barrier to growth.

Rural-urban differences

East Asia is a rapidly urbanising region. However, poverty remains a predominantly rural problem. Across the region, poverty is more pervasive and deeper in rural area. In Vietnam, the rural poor account for almost 90 per cent of total poverty. In the Philippines, poverty is twice as deep in rural areas as in urban centres, rising to three times in Indonesia and Lao PDR, four times in Thailand and ten times in China.

The urban-rural divide is especially marked in China; and it is widening at an accelerating rate. According to World Bank estimates based on Chinese Government data, rural-urban differences accounted for over half of total inequality in 1995, and they explain three-quarters of the increase in inequality since the mid-1980s. By international standards, China's rural-urban income gap is excessive. In most countries, rural incomes are equivalent to two-thirds or more of urban incomes. In China, they are 40 per cent (a decline of one-third since the early 1980s). Taking into account access to subsidised health care, education, and housing, the real gap is much wider, with rural incomes falling to one-third of real urban incomes.

Displacement

Not all of the problems associated with rapid growth are to do with the absence of investment in marginal areas. Some are the direct result of the wrong sort of investment. In the province of Ratnakiri in Cambodia, commercial logging operations and the development of commercial agricultural estates is causing widespread displacement. In Yadao district, Oxfam's partners, who are working with the threatened communities, report that 4,500 people have been displaced in recent months by a 20,000 hectare concession to produce palm oil granted to Malaysian—Cambodian joint-venture. The venture will employ no more than 450 people. Malaysian and Indonesian companies have also been given extensive rights for commercial logging. In 1995, one Indonesian firm was granted a concession of 1.4 million hectares. The potential threat to local communities and the environment on which they depend is enormous. Yet the legal framework for recognising and protecting the rights of indigenous people is lacking.

The concentration of industrial investment in restricted areas has added to the threat of displacement. In the Philippines, the largest of the growth zones being developed under the government's modernisation plan, 'Philippines 2000', links the five provinces of Cavite, Laguna, Batangas, Rizal, and Quezon in the CALABARZON growth zone. Domestic and foreign investors are being provided with huge tax incentives to establish industrial plants in the zone, which they are doing on a large scale. At the southern tip of the zone, in Batangas, the results are evident in spiralling land prices, which have tripled over the past two years. The result: vulnerable communities are being evicted from their land to make way for speculators and assorted projects. According to the Community Extension for Research and Development, an Oxfam International partner which is working with the threatened communities, around 6,000 people are facing eviction in Batangas alone. Many are fisher communities who have been living in the same villages for generations. The same scenario is being played out in thousands of sites across the Philippines and elsewhere in East Asia.

The energy demands created by rapid industrialisation pose a further threat. In China, the National Congress has approved plans to create a dam system on the Yangtze River. The aim is to create 18000MW of electricity, making the scheme the largest-ever hydroelectric project. However, 140 towns and thousands of villages will be flooded, displacing a huge population and destroying a vast area of fertile agricultural land. It is unlikely that the displaced communities will be adequately compensated or provided with alternative sources of livelihood.

Multilateral agencies have often contributed to displacement. In 1989, a World Bank loan supported the Kedung Ombo dam project in Indonesia. This led to the displacement of 30,000 villagers, over two-thirds of whom suffered a direct loss in income as a result. In 1995, an internal World Bank report acknowledged that mistakes had been made and that insufficient attention had been paid to protecting the livelihoods of resettled communities. The incident is not an isolated one. In Thailand, World Bank-funded projects such as the Rubro-Thasase and Pak Moon dams, have become by-words for increasing debt and poverty in the name of 'development'. Looking to the future, the Xiaolangi dam project in China, again funded by the World Bank, threatens to displace 180,000 villagers along the Yellow River. In Lao, the Nam Thuen 2 dam will displace 5000 people.

There is mounting concern in both cases that insufficient attention has been directed towards protecting the livelihoods of those communities who will lose their lands and homes.

Environmental destruction

East Asia has a long history of growth policies which have failed to consider social and environmental costs. Resource-rich countries such as Indonesia, the Philippines, and Malaysia recklessly exploited reserves of timber and minerals to maximise short-term growth. Like the rights of displaced communities, the long-term consequences in terms of lost productivity resulting from soil erosion, siltation, and the destruction of coastal waters, were not recorded in national accounts. The degradation and depletion of natural resources in rural areas has adversely affected the livelihoods of those working in agriculture and fishing, and people dependent on forest products. More recently, the consequences of rapid growth have been apparent in industrial pollution of water and air, often with serious consequences for public health.

Nowhere are the consequences more devastating than in China, where rapid economic growth has been accompanied by equally rapid environmental deterioration. Almost all Chinese cities are now covered by blankets of pollution. In Shenyang and Beijing suspended pollutant particulate volumes are around eight times the WHO safety standard. Of 131 rivers surveyed in 1993, 65 were seriously polluted. Large discharges of industrial pollutants, and pollution accidents (of which around 300 are recorded annually), have added to public health problems. The economic costs of these problems are of enormous dimensions, estimated by the World Bank at around $54bn annually, or the equivalent of 8 per cent of GDP in 1995. The human costs are beyond measurement. They include an estimated 178,000 premature deaths annually in major cities, and blood-lead levels among children averaging 80 per cent higher than those considered dangerous to mental development.

Addressing these problems will require radical policy reforms. Incentives for cleaner and more efficient production technologies, the withdrawal of subsidies and imposition of a pollution tax on coal, and the withdrawal of subsidies on gasoline would all help to encourage more sustainable patterns of industrial development with limited implications for growth and employment creation.

China is not alone in facing an environmental crisis. In Bangkok and Jakarta air pollution is respectively two and four times WHO accepted safety levels. According to a recent World Bank study for Indonesia, the discharge of industrial pollutants will increase ten fold over the next two decades. The same study estimated that the population of Jakarta suffered losses estimated at $500m annually as a result of the health costs of air and water pollution.

Left unchecked, the environmental damage from pollution and the over-extraction of natural resources will undermine the basis for growth with equity in East Asia. Unfortunately, most governments in the region suffer from the 'grow first and clean up the environment later' syndrome. That said, there are some positive signs. Indonesia has phased out subsidies on chemical fertilisers, subsidies on energy inputs have been reduced, and most countries have the savings and investment resources needed to develop cleaner technologies. The next step should be towards full environmental cost-accounting, with governments seeking to ensure, for instance, through tax policies, that producers are penalised for causing environmental damage; and that market prices reflect the wider environmental costs of production.

Inequalities in education

As in other developing regions, poverty in East Asia is strongly correlated with lack of education. This reflects a two-way interaction between education and deprivation. Under-achievement in education reduces income, productivity, and purchasing power. It is also associated with higher levels of vulnerability to sickness, especially among women. Both factors restrict the capacity of poor households to educate their children; and educational under-achievement is one of the most potent factors transmitting poverty across generations. In Vietnam, households in which the head has no formal education are 50 per cent more likely to live in poverty than those where the household head has reached the upper secondary level. In the Philippines, almost three-quarters of those living below the poverty line have either had no formal education, or only primary education. More widely, most East Asian children now have access to at least primary-level education. However, drop-out rates are far higher for low-income groups, while progression rates to secondary education are far lower. In Indonesia, fewer than 10 per cent of the poorest income group progress to secondary education, compared to 75 per cent for the richest income group.

Gender discrimination in education is less pronounced in East Asia than in any other developing region except for Latin America. However, girls suffer some discrimination in terms of education, which results in wider gender inequalities. Overall investments in human capital tend to be higher for boys than for girls, with discrimination becoming more pronounced among poorer families having to make decisions over expenditure in a situation of resource constraint. In China, rural school enrolment is markedly higher for boys than for girls across all age groups, with the gap most pronounced for the 15–19 age group and least pronounced for the 6–9 age group. But a World Bank survey of house-holds in Jiangsu and Sichuan has shown that discrimination against girls weakens at higher income levels, illustrating how household budget constraints increase the disadvantages facing young girls.

Differences in educational attainment, allied to wider social and cultural factors, help to explain male-female income gaps in East Asia. In Korea the gender wage-gap in manufacturing industry has increased dramatically since the 1970s, with female wages now averaging slightly over half of male wages. At the other end of the spectrum, Chinese women typically earn between 80–90 per cent of the wage of their male counterparts. As wage returns to education increase, this gap is likely to widen. Moreover, non-wage forms of discrimination are also important, especially in industries undergoing adjustment pressures. Thus Chinese women are far more likely than men to be laid-off or forced to accept early retirement.

Exploitative labour practices and denial of workers' rights

Rising real wages and the growth of employment have been positive aspects of the East Asian experience. Considerably less positive have been the continued denial of workers' rights, and exploitative labour practices. Most countries in the region restrict basic rights of association and independent trade union action. In Indonesia, China, Thailand, and South Korea, independent trade union leaders are subject to arbitrary arrest, and in some cases torture and lengthy imprisonment. The right to strike is severely curtailed. Women face special problems, ranging from direct wage discrimination to health and safety risks. In countries such as Indonesia, Thailand, and Taiwan, women workers frequently earn between 20-30 per cent less than male counterparts for doing similar work. Labour-intensive industries in Indonesia often recruit female labour — including child labour — from distant rural villages, transferring women to factory compounds.

While most countries have impressive industrial health-and-safety guidelines, these are widely ignored. In 1993 two events cast a shadow over East Asia's export boom. The first was a fire in the Kader factory in Thailand, which killed 188 and injured 469 mainly female workers. The second was another fire, six months later, at the Zhili toy factory in Shenzhen, China, which killed 87 people. Both factories were producing toys for export to the US and Europe — and in both cases health-and-safety standards had been fatally compromised to reduce costs and enhance competitiveness. The incidents were the tip of an iceberg. Each year, thousands of workers are killed or maimed in the booming export industries of China, Indonesia, Thailand, and other countries. Most are women, most are working in factories where even the most basic trade union rights are denied, and most are the victims of policies which allow employers and foreign investors to compromise the safety of workers in the interests of expanding exports.

The increasing mobility of capital has enabled foreign investors to graft the most productive technologies on to highly exploitative labour systems. In Indonesia, the Nike Corporation employs 100,000 people, mostly women, who produce one-third of the company's annual footwear turnover. Basic labour rights are denied and wages are low. In the mining sector foreign investors collude with the government in depriving vulnerable communities of their land rights in order to exploit mineral and forestry resources. Without moves to enhance labour rights and to develop higher standards for foreign investment, East Asian countries are likely to face growing pressures from political coalitions in the industrialised world who regard labour exploitation as being an unacceptable source of competitive advantage.

Indonesia: growth with marginalisation

Indonesia symbolises much that is bad about East Asian development, as well as much that has been good. As we have seen, poverty in Indonesia has declined dramatically along with economic growth; gains in human welfare indicators have been as impressive as economic performance, especially in education and (less so) in health. But there have been limits to the degree of equity achieved. Economic prosperity has been heavily concentrated in parts of Java(centered on Jakarta) and Sumatra (cantered on Riau). In East Nusa Tengarra, the second poorest province in Indonesia, average incomes are one-tenth of those in the richer provinces of Java. Infant mortality rates are twice the national average. Income poverty and low levels of human welfare are made worse by commercial threats to local communities. For example, Oxfam works in East Nusa Tengarra with rural communities who have developed environmentally sustainable agricultural systems which involve rotation and fallowing to prevent soil exhaustion. The Indonesian Government has deemed fallow land to be non-productive and transferred the land rights of farmers to large logging consortia, most of which are linked to senior political figures.

In the area around Bali, large-scale displacements have accompanied the development of the tourist industry. On Lombok, an impoverished island to the east of Bali, companies linked to President Suharto have displaced several hundred households to make way for new hotels. The efforts of these households to secure their rights has come to symbolise a wider struggle for social justice in Indonesia in the face of political and judicial corruption. Tourism provides one example of an industry which creates widespread social marginalisation in the midst of growth. Forestry and mining are others with a similar record. West Kalimantan is one of the richest provinces in Indonesia because of the forestry and commercial agricultural investments which have been attracted over the past two decades. However, the indigenous Dayak people have seen their natural resource base and lands plundered to make way for logging concessions and palm-oil plantations. Forests in which the community previously harvested fruit and rubber have been transferred to corporations, with the government refusing to recognise Dayak land tenure. Protests have been met with political violence, with several thousand lives lost.

Foreign investors have figured prominently in the problems facing marginal communities. The World Development Movement, a British development agency, is campaigning to protect the land rights of the Aumngwe people of West Papua. The threat comes from Rio Tinto Zinc, a British company which is investing $700m in expanding the Grasberg open-cast copper and gold mine The Amungwe and other indigenous people are now threatened by displacement from their ancestral lands. Yet their land rights are unacknowledged either by the Indonesian Government, or by the investor concerned.

Social policy roots of economic problems

There are warning signs that social policy is in urgent need of renewal in a number of East Asian countries. This applies especially to Indonesia and Thailand, two of the three countries at the centre of the recent crisis in foreign currency markets. The Philippines, the third country, does not merit inclusion in the East Asian success story, but it too is a testament to the economic consequences of poor social policies, having subjected its education system to gross neglect. In all three countries, the recent slowdown in economic growth and associated currency problems are associated with failures in social policy.

Both Indonesia and Thailand have made major advances in education, achieving near-universal primary school enrolment and near-universal literacy for young age groups. However, Thailand has the lowest secondary school enrolment rate in the region, closely followed by Indonesia. Moreover, Indonesia spends a good deal less than other countries on education as a percentage of GDP — less than one-third the next lowest country, which is the Philippines. As a percentage of budget allocations, Indonesia spends less than one quarter as much as countries such as Malaysia and Korea. The consequences are reflected in poor quality education and high drop-out rates. While over 90 per cent of the population start primary school, almost one-third fail to finish. Drop-out rates are higher for girls than boys, although this gender difference is narrowing. The real gender gap is revealed in the fact that 25 per cent of girls receive no schooling: twice the proportion of boys.

How has inadequate investment in education contributed to the present crisis? First, both Indonesia and Thailand have experienced serious bottlenecks for skilled labour, hampering efforts to attract investment in more sophisticated, higher-value-added areas of production. In neither country has social policy prepared the way for the transition to higher levels of economic development in the way that it did for the transition from agriculture to labour-intensive industrialisation. This has raised questions about whether export growth can be sustained in the longer term. Second, failure to climb the technological ladder has left Indonesia and Thailand facing intense competition for foreign investment from countries such as China and Vietnam where wages are lower.

Failure to progressively raise levels of education and human development will raise the spectre of a growing number of countries becoming locked into low-wage competition, with standards being driven down towards the lowest level, across the region. The challenge is to improve the quality of social provision and access to it. However, efforts to improve quality are hampered by the failure of governments to respond to public demands. In the cases of China and Vietnam, the public have responded by voting with their feet, bypassing state services in favour of private-sector providers. This trend is contributing to growing inequality since the poor are unable to afford private options.

7 Postcript: The East Asian crisis and the threat to growth with equity

Uniquely in the developing world, East Asia has succeeded in combining sustained and rapid economic growth with stability. Central banking authorities have played a crucial role in maintaining low inflation and the stable exchange rates which are essential to export success. Contrasts between the 'smoothly adjusting' experience of East Asia and the roller-coaster of hyper-inflation and devaluation in Latin America have become the stuff of text-book macro-economics. At the end of 1997, such contrasts appear less marked. East Asia's economies have been rocked by a succession of financial crises, culminating in the largest-ever international financial rescue operation carried out under IMF auspices.

Underlying causes of the crisis

Several factors have combined to cause the recent turmoil in East Asian markets. First, global demand for some of East Asia's most important exports has slowed, especially in the electronics and semi-conductor sectors. Overall export growth in 1996 fell to 5 per cent, from 22 per cent the previous year. Second, the US dollar, to which most East Asian currencies are tied, has appreciated by some 50 per cent against the yen, undermining export competitiveness and driving up imports.[199] Countries such as Thailand, which were less flexible in their response to shifting currency alignments, have suffered the most intensive adjustment pressures. Current-account deficits have widened to alarming levels in some countries. While there is no benchmark for a sustainable current account, deficits in excess of 5 per cent of national income are a source for concern in almost any situation. The Philippines and Indonesia are approaching this mark; Thailand has gone far beyond it, with a deficit equivalent to 7 per cent of national income.[200]

Policy makers in all three countries have turned a blind eye to the impending crisis for at least three years. Investment levels have been high, but an increasing share of activity has been concentrated in speculation rather than production. Property markets and stock exchanges have boomed, acting as a magnet for foreign capital. Within this broad picture, the precise circumstances have differed from country to country. In Malaysia, a decline in the *quality* of growth has been apparent since the early 1990s, with the country's ascent up the manufacturing value-added ladder slowing, along with growth in productivity. To compensate, the government has taken the lead in promoting investment, embarking on ever-more-grandiose development projects. The world's tallest building, the Petronas Tower and a new administrative centre at Putrajaya (costing $8bn at pre-crisis exchange rates) are two such projects. A third was the Baku dam, which ranks as one of the most costly and least efficient power projects in the developing world, with projected costs estimated at $7bn. These investments sucked in vast quantities of imports, financed in part by an unregulated credit boom. By the end of 1997, Malaysia had achieved one of the world's highest investment rates (equivalent to 43 per cent of GDP), and a domestic-loans-to-GDP rate of 170 per cent — the highest in South-East Asia. As the surge in credit pulled in imports and concentrated investments into projects with shrinking returns, the current-account deficit widened and the real economy became increasingly divorced from the speculative economy.[201]

In Thailand, credit expansion was linked to global finance markets, as local companies and financial institutions built up dollar debt while interest rates were low, re-lending the money to fund a boom in real estate and speculative stocks.[202] Thus, while Malaysia's debt problems are rooted in the domestic banking system, Thailand has emerged with a foreign debt crisis. In the two years to 1996, foreign borrowing by Thai financial institutions doubled to $77bn. As the current-account deficit widened in the face of the fall in exports, and the government turned to high interest-rates to maintain the value of the baht, a financial crisis swiftly ensued. Manufacturing sectors were also hit hard by the rise in interest rates, with unemployment levels rising and output falling. Thailand's foreign-exchange reserves were depleted by an ultimately unsuccessful effort to fend off devaluation.

As in the run-up to Mexico's financial collapse (see below), the combination of heavy foreign capital inflows and weak financial regulation allowed lenders in many East Asian countries to expand credit, often to risky borrowers, making the financial system as a whole more vulnerable. The Philippines, Indonesia, and — less spectacularly — Malaysia have all followed Thailand in devaluing their currencies. In each case, the combination of speculation, rising foreign and domestic debt, and a slow-down in exports has been in evidence.

The deepest problems are unfolding in Indonesia, which is on the brink of a fully-fledged debt crisis. Between 1993 and 1996, Indonesia's foreign debt increased from $90bn to $105bn. With growth in exports slowing and debt servicing already absorbing one-quarter of export earnings, serious external debt problems loom for the first time in 20 years. Today, Indonesia's foreign debt has climbed to almost $140bn, with private companies accounting for $80bn of the total, and government debt the remainder. At the lowest point in the exchange rate with the dollar, Indonesia had an external debt equivalent to 192 per cent of GDP. A major problem for Indonesia is that the bulk of private debt is short-term. Some $67bn in repayments are scheduled for the first half of 1998, while the current-account surplus is projected at only $8bn. In effect, this means that much of the private sector is bankrupt, with devaluation having exposed an unsustainable debt-profile. According to Pentosenaa Securities, one of the most respected brokerage houses in Jakarta, only 22 of the 282 companies listed on the stock exchange now have sufficient cash-flow to meet their debt obligations.[203] Most of these 22 companies are exporters in areas such as palm oil, fisheries, and petroleum, whereas industries relying on the domestic market — such as paper-mills, shoes and textiles manufactures, and construction — are highly prone to bankruptcy. Unless their debt problems can be resolved, mass unemployment will occur. However, Indonesia's debts are harder to deal with than those of, say, South Korea. This is because loans were channelled through a plethora of borrowers, rather than a limited number of banks. As in Malaysia and Thailand, the decoupling of investment from the productive economy, and the associated speculative activity, pose the threat of high adjustment costs through enforced devaluation.

Events in Thailand, Indonesia, and the Philippines were a prelude to the crisis which engulfed South Korea in November, 1997. News that the country was turning to the IMF for a bail-out package led to a sharp devaluation and drove share prices to their lowest level since 1987.[204] As with its neighbouring 'tigers', the problems of South Korea were rooted in domestic debt and mismanagement of the banking system, with basic banking principles subordinated to the pursuit of vested interests. Simply stated, the *chaebol*, the giant conglomerates which dominate South Korea's economy, had been allowed to borrow too much in relation to their capacity to repay. The habit of allocating funds through political *diktat,* rather than on the basis of proper risk assessment, contributed to a situation in which firms could borrow without regard for their capacity to generate adequate returns. Inefficient use of credit left the *chaebol* with debts equivalent to four times the value of their equity. Such ratios proved inherently unsustainable when rates of growth slowed at home and abroad. Almost all of Korea's 50 largest firms are massively over-burdened with debt. The extent of the crisis was obscured by a complex system of cross-subsidisation, mutual payment guarantees (under which companies provide surety to third-party lenders), inter-corporate loans, and opaque accounting procedures. In effect, the *chaebol* were linked in a system built on financial insolvency, creating a devastating domino effect when the full extent of the crisis emerged. When the country's twelfth-largest *chaebol,* Halla, collapsed with debts of $5bn (20 times its equity), it emerged that Hyundai (owned by the brother of its senior executive) accounted for 15 per cent of its debt.[205] With the top four *chaebol* (Hyundai, Daewoo, LG, and Samsung) accounting for over half of the country's exports, their financial mismanagement and poor performance threatened — and delivered — a wider economic disaster.

Initially, South Korea appeared to be facing a classic liquidity crisis in domestic markets. It rapidly emerged, however, that external-debt mismanagement had introduced a foreign-exchange element into the crisis. As the domestic debt situation worsened, the government colluded with the *chaebol* heads to authorise increased short-term borrowing overseas. Short-term loans, repayable in dollars, were used to finance long-term debt denominated in won. The full extent of overseas borrowing was systematically obscured. By December 1997, it emerged that the country's external dollar-denominated debt stood at $100bn, compared to earlier official figures suggesting $65bn. Evidence of the scale of the problem resulted in a 30 per cent devaluation of the won, driving up the costs of debt repayment. Early indications are that the resources mobilised by the IMF will be insufficient to halt the slide and restore confidence, leaving Western governments to consider an even larger support package, or to accept the likely consequence of inaction: namely, economic collapse and a political explosion.

In each of these cases, the causes of the financial crisis can be traced to economic fundamentals. Unsustainable debt-to-sales ratios in the private sector, unregulated credit expansion, foreign-debt mismanagement, exchange-rate misalignment, and large current-account deficits all figure, to varying degrees.

Yet important as these problems were, they were in one sense symptomatic of wider political failures. In South Korea, the *chaebol* and the major banks were, with government collusion, able to obscure the scale of debt. When Thailand's new Finance Minister, Thanong Bidaya, assumed office in June 1997, the country's officially reported foreign-exchange reserves stood at $30bn. In fact, that figure was a myth. The real figure was $1.2bn — equivalent to just two days' worth of imports. [206] Politically directed misreporting, and unreported subsidisation by the central bank and by finance houses controlled by members of the cabinet and powerful families, had concealed the true position. In Indonesia, the entire banking and finance system has been structured around private vested interests, with political directions rather than sound banking principles determining lending policies. In each case, and at every level, unaccountability in politics, and the absence of independent public scrutiny, informed public debate, and a critical press, enabled financial mismanagement and corruption to continue unchallenged. This under-lines the importance of building economic reform on new political structures.

The IMF as a lender-of-last-resort

Whatever its various causes, the crisis in East Asia has posed unprecedented new threats to the global financial system, sending shock waves to Wall Street, Europe, and Latin America. In Brazil, the government has been forced to revise its public spending and taxation plans in the direction of increased austerity in an effort to maintain financial stability and protect the domestic banking system. Growth forecasts for the global economy are being revised downwards on an almost daily basis. The OECD has reduced the projected growth rate for its members for 1998 by 1 per cent (to 2.5 per cent).[207]

In the recent past, political interest in East Asia in the industrialised world has focused on the threat posed by the region's exports to employment and livelihoods. In the near future, that threat may shift to the employment consequences of a slow-down in East Asia, with its corollary of lost export markets. Recognition of the severity of East Asia's financial crisis, and a concern to limit its contagion effects, has resulted in an unprecedented international rescue effort. Over $100bn has been mobilised so far by the industrialised countries, $35bn of it within the IMF, which has massively over-extended itself in East Asia.[208] In South Korea, the Fund is providing $21bn (out of $57bn), breaking the record for its previous largest loan, given to Mexico in 1995. In Indonesia, IMF contributions amount to $10bn out of a $27bn package. In the case of Thailand, the IMF's involvement is a more modest, but still significant, $4bn. Apart from its own resources, the IMF effectively governs access to the national resources provided by governments since its imprimatur is a standing requirement for all of the East Asian countries seeking assistance.

In effect, the East Asian crisis has become the first test-case for the international mechanisms created after the Mexican crisis to contain future problems in global financial markets. After that crisis, the IMF was established as a global lender-of-last-resort, with a new facility — the New Agreement to Borrow — established to underpin its operations. Its massive policy influence in East Asia now derives not only from its financial weight and the resources it is able to mobilise directly, but also from its role as a gatekeeper for support from other creditors.

The Mexican path to low growth and high inequality

The case of Mexico graphically illustrates the differences between East Asia and Latin America.[209] It also illustrates the potential threats posed by the current financial crisis in East Asia to the prospects for continued growth with equity.

During the 1990s, Mexico has been a model liberalising economy. The country has embarked upon one of the largest privatisation programmes in history, financial markets have been opened up, and trade liberalisation has been accelerated through the North American Free Trade Agreement (NAFTA) and commitments to the WTO. By the early 1990s, almost 90 per cent of imports fell into the liberalised category. Over $11bn in direct foreign investment entered the country in 1994 alone, as foreign companies developed their operations in the country's *maquiladora* zone on the US border.

Even before the slump which followed the financial crash of 1994, economic growth was slow at 2.1 per cent per annum: lower than the average rate during the 'lost decade' of the 1980s. Real wages remained static and unemployment rose slightly. In rural areas, the number of people living in poverty continued to rise, increasing from 6.7 million in 1989 to 8.8 million in 1993. At the other end of the spectrum, vast fortunes were made from the opportunities created by privatisation and financial deregulation. During the first half of the 1990s, the number of dollar billionaires in Mexico rose from 10 to 15. By 1996, the combined wealth of these billionaires was equivalent to about 9 per cent of Mexico's GDP.

As in other Latin American countries, wealthy people in Mexico are not inclined to save and invest. Their preference for consumption is reflected in Mexico's savings rates of 15 per cent of GDP, less than half the average for East Asia. As a result, such growth as occurred was converted not into investment, which actually fell between 1991 and 1995, but consumption. Imports flooded into the country, creating a huge current-account deficit. By 1994, the deficit had climbed to 7 per cent of GDP, higher than it was at the onset of the debt crisis. An over-valued exchange rate exacerbated the problem by artificially reducing the price of the imports consumed by the middle-class, while reducing the competitiveness of exports. Unwilling to devalue the currency, the Government chose to finance the trade deficit by attracting speculative capital from Europe and the US, issuing bonds at progressively higher interest rates. The bubble burst at the end of 1994, when it became apparent that the government would be unable to finance repayments on the $28bn in bonds held by foreigners.

Financial collapse was averted by a hastily contrived rescue package under which the IMF committed $18bn to Mexico (three times the country's borrowing entitlement) and the US a further $50bn. The loans were advanced at market interest rates under strict repayment conditions which demanded drastic cuts in public spending. Having been bypassed by the consumer boom of the first half of the 1990s, Mexico's poor have spent the second half paying for its consequences. More than one million people lost their jobs as the domestic economy contracted by 8 per cent and investment fell by 40 per cent. Real wages fell by over 30 per cent. Meanwhile, the already weakened social safety-net effectively disintegrated as social-sector budgets were cut.

Much has been made of the 'success' of the Mexican financial rescue package. Economic growth reached 4 per cent in 1996 and exports are booming. The country's debt to the US and the IMF has been repaid, several months ahead of time. Seen from the perspective of Mexico's poor, the success is less apparent. Wages will not recover their pre-collapse value until after 2000, and unemployment continues to affect around one-quarter of the workforce. Recovery has been for the most part confined to the export sector, which now accounts for over one-quarter of GDP. The problem is that the export sector itself is highly concentrated, with some 600 companies accounting for 80 per cent of exports. Most of these companies, especially those in the *maquiladora* zone, have weak links to the domestic economy, which explains the slow rate of job creation.

The IMF intervention in East Asia

One of the reasons for the political resentment now being directed at the Fund in East Asia is that it is seen as having usurped the role of governments. In countries which pride themselves on their self-reliance and financial independence, that resentment is understandable, but of questionable relevance. Under almost any conditions, gross financial mismanagement has unfortunate consequences, one of which is a loss of power to creditors. No amount of populist rhetoric about the violation of sovereignty can hide the extent of mismanagement which has taken place. That said, the excessive secrecy surrounding IMF operations has generated justified concern over the erosion of democracy and accountability.

This raises an issue which goes beyond East Asia's problems to the heart of global governance. As the IMF's power expands, so the need to subject the agency to more effective public scrutiny, and to improve the flow of information which it provides, becomes more urgent. At present, the IMF is a law unto itself, as its recent interventions in East Asia under-line. With the partial exception of Indonesia, the conditions attached to its loans are unknown, except to a small group of technocrats.[210] Citizens in countries receiving these loans have a right to know these conditions, and the Letters of Intent and other documents in which they are set out should be made publicly available.

Looking beyond questions of accountability, there are two broader yardsticks against which the Fund's actions must be judged. The first concerns the appropriateness of its policy advice for the task of restoring stability and growth. The second is the imperative of ensuring that the poor do not bear an undue share of the burden of adjustment. On current form, the Fund is failing abysmally on both counts.

Some of the difficulties with the IMF's intervention can be traced to basic principles. Just as it did in Latin America in the 1980s, the Fund has assumed that foreign creditor demands should be met in full in order to restore what it euphemistically describes as 'confidence'. The under-lying economic rationale, which dictates that foreign investors who have recklessly engaged in high-risk lending should be bailed out at public expense, is unclear. By insulating such investors from risk, the Fund is creating a moral hazard: in effect, encouraging other investors to engage in similarly reckless action on the assumption that they too will be insulated from risk. This poses a threat to the stability of the global financial system. More immediately, it opens the IMF to the charge that it places the interests of Wall Street above the interests of the poor, upon whom the costs of converting private debt into public property fall when the Fund provides a 'rescue' operation.

As suggested by the analysis above, East Asia's problems are rooted in grossly inefficient financial systems, combined (in Thailand's case) with foreign-exchange mismanagement. High inflation and fiscal profligacy are not part of the problem. Thailand has a fiscal surplus (i.e government revenues exceed spending), while both Indonesia and South Korea have balanced budgets. Whatever their difficulties, East Asian countries are not facing the same problems as those which engulfed Latin America in the 1980s, when rampant inflation and unsustainable budgets were the order of the day. Still less is East Asia in the same boat as the highly indebted countries of Africa, which have been a focus of the IMF's policy work since the early 1980s.

Yet despite the underlying economic differences, East Asia has been prescribed a classic dose of debt deflation on the Latin American model.[211] Monetary and fiscal policy has been tightened to the point of strangulation, threatening to kill the patient during the first phase of treatment. For instance, in South Korea, the IMF wants to see interest rates more than doubled to 15 per cent in real terms (i.e. above the rate of inflation). This will inevitably lead to the early collapse of many companies, resulting in a loss of production and employment opportunities. Bankruptcies have already risen to record levels, with over 2,000 small and medium-sized enterprises collapsing each month since the rescue package was adopted. Investor confidence, domestic and foreign, is also likely to crumble in the face of high interest rates and the wholesale collapse of enterprises which could, through loan restructuring, become commercially viable.

Intense fiscal pressures are also being applied in Thailand, where public spending is to be reduced by the equivalent of 3 per cent of GDP. In Indonesia, public spending is scheduled to fall by around 10 per cent. Initially, the IMF's conditions for loans to both countries included the requirement that they achieve budget surpluses equivalent to 1 per cent of GDP. This requirement has now been relaxed in the face of deepening threats of a full-scale recession in both countries, with broadly balanced budgets now required. The same applies to South Korea. However, even these less stringent targets remain inappropriate. The crisis in East Asia has been caused by a combination of weak financial systems, unwise private-sector lending, and huge inflows of private capital, not by fiscal mismanagement. Given the region's high levels of savings and the soundness of public finances, there is far greater scope for prudent public spending to create a more expansionary environment. Above all, this is

135

needed to address the problem of mass unemployment. The scale of the threat in this area is not sufficiently appreciated by the IMF and other creditors.

In Thailand, official estimates suggest that unemployment has risen by over 40 per cent, to 1.7 million, over the past six months — and that another 2 million will be added to this figure in 1998. Projections for Indonesia are even more disturbing. At the end of 1997, open unemployment in Jakarta stood at 7 per cent, compared to 4 per cent in 1996. This represents 4.4 million people. According to the Manpower Ministry, the number affected by unemployment will rise to 6 million by the end of 1998.[212] Other projections put the figure closer to 9 million. Much will depend on the fate of the estimated 1.4 million Indonesians working in Malaysia, many of them illegally. Mass repatriations have already started, with the Malaysian government announcing, in December 1997, its intention to expel 850,000 foreign workers. What is already clear is that the rapid expansion of employment and rising real wages which have driven poverty reduction in East Asia have ended. In Indonesia, growth rates of 5 per cent are needed just to absorb the 2.5 million new entrants coming into the labour market each year. Growth projections for 1998 are less than 1 per cent, compared to 7 per cent in 1996. In South Korea, the down-turn is likely to be less dramatic, with a growth rate of 2 per cent likely. Even so, unemployment will increase by over 1 million.

There is a growing belief among economists that the IMF, with the endorsement of the US, is being over-zealous in its demands for deflation. The fear is that a vicious cycle of economic decline will gather momentum, with damaging social consequences. In contrast to earlier periods of employment and income growth, a period of weakening demand, falling wages, and growing unemployment, could reduce investment and output, and further increase unemployment, potentially giving rise to violent forms of protest. Part of the difficulty in assessing the Fund's approach derives from the excessive secrecy surrounding its operations.[213] While the Fund is justified in pointing out that there is no pain-free option in dealing with a financial crisis,[214] there is scope for debate on the pace and sequencing of reforms. Unfortunately, governments of the industrialised countries appear to regard IMF prescriptions as unquestionable truths — an approach which is made more difficult to understand given the Fund's long history of failure in managing debt problems.

Whatever the appropriateness or otherwise of the fiscal conditions attached to IMF loans, other aspects of conditionality, formal and informal, are even less defensible than the obsession with deflation and fiscal austerity. For instance, the Fund has argued for accelerated financial liberalisation in Indonesia, Thailand, and South Korea, including the withdrawal of regulations on the sale of debt and equity to foreign corporations. It also insists that foreign banks be allowed in immediately, with the right to acquire majority stakes in local banks and purchase assets as they see fit. Both demands carry the very heavy imprint of US influence over the IMF, increasing concern that the Fund is being used as the bilateral arm of US trade policy. American manipulation aside, deregulation of the financial system is the last thing that is needed under the present circumstances. With banking, property, and equity markets in turmoil, effective regulation should be a first priority. Moreover, deregulation under existing conditions would enable foreign companies to purchase stocks for next-to-nothing, with corporate profit being enhanced in a manner which imposes long-term costs on the local economy.

What is required is a more considered analysis of the underlying problems which have afflicted East Asia's banking systems. The received wisdom within the IMF and most Western governments is that the region has suffered the consequences of financial protectionism, hence the emphasis on capital-account liberalisation. To the extent that this is geared towards the promotion of long-term financing, it may be justified. Yet East Asia's main failing was not that it liberalised too little, but that it liberalised too far and too fast in the wrong areas, and without adequate regulation.

In one sense, the crisis has been an outgrowth of the East Asian 'model'. High levels of savings, amounting to over one-third of GDP, have been transferred to banks, which acted as intermediaries to the corporate sector. The result: a high ratio of bank liability to GDP, and equally high levels of debt in relation to corporate assets.[215] While risky, this situation can sustain a high growth path, provided that the resulting investment raises productivity in the real economy. The problems in East Asia began when banks began to lend recklessly on property and grandiose construction projects, with the banking system itself debased to the status of what *The Economist* described as 'little better than political piggy-banks'.[216] Up to a third of the assets of many of the largest banks in Thailand, Indonesia, and Malaysia were directed to this purpose by 1997. The impact of this error was compounded by the involvement of foreign lenders. Bankers and governments assumed that they could borrow indefinitely in dollars to buy assets in local currency. They also took it for granted that stable exchange rates would continue, failing to guard against the possibility of devaluation. The mistake was in the political decision not only to tolerate a credit-induced speculative boom in

137

property, but to fuel it by encouraging increasingly short-term borrowing at unrealistically high exchange rates. For fragile and narrow financial systems in which relatively small amounts of inflows from global markets can have disproportionately large effects, short-term borrowing from foreign lenders poses inevitable risks. For countries with savings rates as high as those in East Asia, such risks are unnecessary and unjustified.[217] Ultimately, losses incurred in the domestic banking system as a result of reckless short-term borrowing are absorbed in public finance, which is why control over foreign capital flows, allied to prudential banking regulations, is inescapable.

Unjustified as the IMF's efforts to promote capital-market liberalisation are, the attempts being made by the Fund and the US to use financial conditionality as a lever for trade liberalisation are even less justified. The US is pressing Indonesia to reduce agricultural import-controls on rice and other basic commodities. Once again, the potential benefits to US companies from enhanced market access are high. However, trade liberalisation would have the effect of eroding the market interventions which have been so successful in reducing rural poverty. In Indonesia, the reduction of import controls on wheat could result in local markets being flooded by cheap imports from the US. In South Korea, recent government moves to liberalise car imports have been traced directly to US pressure, effected through the mediation of the IMF. Such issues, along with those concerning the opening up of financial sectors, are properly dealt with under the auspices of the WTO rather than in the context of IMF rescue operations.

It is clearly unacceptable for the IMF to be used as the thin end of the wedge for the pursuit of US commercial interests. That said, many of the reforms which the Fund has attempted to negotiate are long overdue. For instance, new structures are being created to increase the independence of central banks, with South Korea and Thailand having introduced significant reforms to this end. IMF staff are also involved in dialogue aimed at improving financial management, with an emphasis on the creation of proper accounting and reporting procedures. In Indonesia, some of the reforms demanded by the Fund strike at the heart of the systems of corruption and patronage revolving around the President.[218] Twelve major infrastructure projects have been axed, including the massive Tanjung Jati-C power plant, many of them linked to the President's family.

State support for the national car company owned by President Suharto's son has also been withdrawn, and a lucrative monopoly on the purchase of cloves owned by the same son has been withdrawn. State funding for an aircraft manufacturing plant controlled by one Presidential political ally has been terminated, as has the timber cartel controlled by another. If carried through, these measures could have important redistributive benefits, releasing public finance for investment in priority social areas. Similarly, the removal of domestic marketing restrictions could help to raise rural incomes. Producers of cloves, cashew nuts, vanilla, and oranges are now free to trade across district and provincial boundaries, and export taxes are being lowered. But perhaps the most important innovation of all has been the IMF's insistence on publishing its Letters of Intent with Indonesia — the document which sets out the broad terms and conditions attached to its loan. This action will not only enhance public debate in Indonesia itself, but will also go some way towards improving the IMF's own transparency.

Not all of the problems associated with implementation of the rescue packages can be laid at the door of the IMF. Political elites in the region have been highly effective in protecting their interests. In South Korea, political influence from the *chaebol* resulted in two of the country's worst-managed and chronically over-extended banks being nationalised rather than closed, as called for by the IMF.[219] In effect, powerful corporate interests have been able to force the state and public finance to accept responsibility for their private debt. In Indonesia, the banks earmarked for closure appear to have been carefully selected to avoid costs to members of President Suharto's family. Admittedly, the closure of the Bambang Trihatmodjo bank, owned by the President's son, briefly raised hopes that some semblance of technocratic discipline had been restored, only for a new bank to emerge in the same office under the same management auspices within a matter of weeks.[220]

Implications for the poor: the missing agenda

Failure to adopt more balanced approaches to conditionality will inevitably inflame political passions in East Asia. Other issues should already be inflaming passions. As the IMF and its growing band of critics argue over the technical details of the rescue operations, the voice of those who will feel the most pain is conspicuous by its absence. The implications of the present crisis for the poor, and for poverty reduction, have yet to be established on the policy agenda, let alone as a consideration in guiding policy choices. This too carries echoes from the Latin American debt crisis, when the interests of the poor were disregarded in the pursuit of financial stabilisation targets. Today, there are more impoverished people in that region than there were at the start of the debt crisis in 1980, suggesting powerful lessons for East Asia.

Coverage of the crisis in East Asia to date has been dominated by problems in financial markets. Not enough has been heard about the social consequences of economic decline; and not enough thought has been given to addressing these consequences. Perhaps three decades of strong growth and progress towards poverty reduction has obscured the fact that one in ten Indonesians — some 20 million people — live below the $1-a-day poverty line. Probably as many again live just above it. In Thailand, absolute poverty has almost been eradicated, but around 6 million Thais live on between $1 and $2 a day, precariously close to the poverty line. Elsewhere in the region, the crisis will have powerful transmission effects; for instance, as recession in Thailand results in the repatriation of workers from Burma.

Field reports from Oxfam International partners working with vulnerable communities in East Asia are already starting to point to serious increases in poverty. Consider the case, summarised in one recent report, of Phyllis Domingues, a smallholder farmer and mother of four living in West Nussa Tengarra, one of the most deprived areas in Indonesia. Until November 1997, she used to receive the equivalent of around $15 from a brother working in Jakarta. This supplemented the income from agriculture and the sale of *ikat*, a locally produced cloth, financing about one-third of the household's spending. Phyllis Domingues' ability to purchase food, clothing, education, and health services has depended critically on the remittances from her brother. Today, however, her brother is unemployed, having lost his job in a factory producing iron rods for the construction sector. Asked how she will cope, Ms Domingues responds: 'How can we cope? The choice is simple: we eat less, or we take the children out of school. Which choice would you make?'

Accounts of individual hardship should not be dismissed as unrepresentative anecdote; the dilemma faced by Phyllis Domingues is one being faced with increasing frequency across Indonesia and other countries in the region. There are around 3 million migrants from impoverished rural communities in the Outer Islands now working in or around Jakarta. Many thousands more have been working in Malaysia and Thailand. Remittances from these migrant workers provide income for around one in three households. Today, however, this vital stream of income is drying up. Thousands of Indonesian migrant workers are being sent home from Malaysia and Thailand as the economic crisis deepens there. Many thousands more are losing their jobs in Jakarta. For each of these jobs lost, there is a multiplier effect in rural villages, as households are forced to reduce consumption and withdraw children from school. In areas such as East Nussa Tengarra, Irian Jaya, and West Kalimantan, where poverty incidence exceeds 40 per cent, the human welfare costs will be severe. Equally severe will be an increase in urban poverty. There is already evidence of squatter settlements expanding across Jakarta, and this trend will continue.

The same tragedy is being played out in Thailand. In the rural north-east, where over half of the absolute poor live, poverty levels are rising in the face of lost remittances. Meanwhile, deepening urban poverty is adding massively to pressures on poor households. The threat of mass unemployment fuelling the country's prostitution industry looms large, as does the prospect of women being forced into increasingly hazardous and low-paid sections of the informal economy. Even in relatively prosperous South Korea, the absence of a functioning welfare state will result in unprecedented hardship in the face of mass unemployment. It is far from certain that the social and political fabric of the country will survive intact.

Reductions in public spending could act as a further driving force for poverty, reducing the basic services available to the poor at precisely the time when the need for them is increasing. The immediate consequences will be registered in the form of reduced opportunities for education and diminished access to health facilities. In the longer term, public spending cuts could sever the link which has been established between growth and equity, to the detriment of both. For instance, Thailand's economic problems are related to a deepening skills-shortage in sectors vital for the transition to a more diverse and technologically sophisticated economy. Deteriorating educational performance will undermine prospects for such a transition. In Indonesia, cuts in public spending could exacerbate existing inadequacies in the health system, notably with regard to the under-provisioning for women's health care.

There are plenty of other candidates for public spending cuts. Grandiose infrastructure projects abound, as do political 'kick-back' funds associated with them. The postponement of the Baku dam project in Malaysia and the 12 major infrastructure projects listed for cancellation in the IMF loan package to Indonesia are steps in the right direction. It is fully justified for the IMF to demand that extravagant projects and subsidies for elites are cut before priority services for the poor; indeed, equally strict conditionality should be applied for the protection of these services. Unpopular as it would doubtless be politically with powerful elites, this is one area in which creditor influence could play a useful role.

While some pressure on public spending is inevitable, governments and the IMF have a responsibility to ensure that the basic services used by the poor are protected. The World Bank has an important role to play in this area. It is providing significant resources (around $16bn) to the rescue packages for South Korea, Indonesia, and Thailand, with around $1bn earmarked for social-sector programmes. These will take the form of urban and rural social funds, and programmes to protect access to basic health and education services.[221]

National and international action to end instability

For some political leaders in East Asia, the current crisis is the work solely of ruthless currency speculators. Populist rhetoric to this effect has provided a convenient smokescreen for obscuring the policy failures of governments. That said, speculative investments, and currency trading in pursuit of quick profits, have contributed to the crisis in East Asia, just as they did in Mexico. Financial deregulation, the weakening of currency controls, and inadequate regulation of stock markets has created a climate in which speculative activity, domestic and foreign, has flourished. Domestic policy reforms alone will be unable to address these problems, which are linked to the globalisation of world capital and currency markets. The deregulation of these markets, cheap tele-communications, the development of a wide range of financial derivative products, and instant access to markets through electronic trading, has fundamentally shifted the balance of power between governments and speculators in favour of the latter. Daily turnover on foreign exchanges has reached $1.2 trillion dollars, equivalent to around one-quarter of annual world trade flows, and only slightly less than the assets held by the world's central banks. Currency markets now represent a concentration of financial power to which even the world's richest countries are vulnerable.

During the 1992 Exchange Rate Mechanism crisis in Europe, some $130bn was mobilised in an unsuccessful attempt to protect the British pound and other currencies against speculation.[222] More recently, currency speculation in East Asia has compounded the destabilising effects of the region's financial problems, with countries such as Thailand, Malaysia, and the Philippines seeing their foreign currency reserves eliminated in vain efforts by central banks to protect their values.

Can anything be done to contain the speculative power of money markets? Perhaps the most effective action is for governments to maintain realistic currency alignments. One of the lessons of the 1990s is that governments which seek to maintain over-valued exchange rates will pay a high price, exposing their economies to speculative attack. To different degrees, Britain and Thailand both paid a high price for exchange-rate mismanagement, creating the opportunity for currency traders to gamble on the inevitable devaluation.

But while it may be the case that sound policies limit the scope for currency speculation, the increasing volatility of exchange rates has led to the danger of economic disruption, with uncertainty threatening to undermine productive investment and diminish trade performance. This is especially true for developing countries, where resource limitations create particularly high levels of vulnerability. Ironically, the international financier and currency speculator, George Soros, who is blamed by the Malaysian government for causing the country's recent currency crisis, has been among the most articulate advocates of the case for controls on currency markets, repeatedly warning governments of the need to protect their economies through regulation.[223] He has also argued for the creation of an International Credit Insurance Corporation as a sister institution to the IMF. This new body would guarantee international loans for a modest fee, with borrowing countries obliged to provide data on all borrowings, public and private. Ceilings would be set on the amount the institution insured, based on this data and on wider macro-economic conditions.[224]

Arguments, such as those advanced by George Soros, in favour of regulation are steadily gaining ground, not least within the international financial community. The collapse of fixed-exchange-rate regimes in East Asia has confronted governments with the threat of systemic collapse, with financial melt-down in the region impacting on the global economy. Some commentators, including the former US Labour Secretary, Robert Reich, now point to ominous parallels with the 1930s.[225] Over-stated as this warning may be, the 'contagion' effects of the East Asian crisis are readily apparent. Financial markets in Latin America have been destabilised, the crisis in the Japanese banking system (which is heavily exposed in East Asia) has deepened, and commodity prices are in decline. What can be done to avert future crises?

Action to reduce currency speculation is a necessary, if insufficient, requirement. During one bout of populist rhetoric, the Malaysian Prime Minister, Marahir Mohammed, denounced currency trading as 'unnecessary, unproductive, and immoral'.[226] Whatever the judgement on the third count, he was right on the first two. The problem is that currency speculators now have the power to destabilise entire economies, and that the global currency system has been decoupled from the global productive system. One of the most effective ways to achieve realignment would be to tax speculative activity, for instance through currency transaction taxes. A uniform tax on foreign exchange transactions of around 0.25 per cent would be sufficient to erode the small margins and currency alignment shifts exploited by speculators.[227] The incidence of taxation would fall heaviest on yields from short 'round trips', where speculators send a portfolio of currencies around the world stopping off *en route* to take speculative profits. Long-term direct foreign investment would be relatively unaffected. Governments in Europe, Latin America, and now East Asia have all suffered heavily at the hands of currency speculators, and share a common interest in adopting a tax measure designed to curtail their power. That said, governments bent on maintaining either heavily over-valued or under-valued currencies will remain vulnerable to speculative attack.

Turning from currency speculation to banking and finance, action is needed at the national level in both the developed and the developing world. Attractive as the Soros proposal for an International Credit Insurance Corporation is to the financial community, not least because it would effectively provide a public guarantee for private investment, it is no substitute for effective action by governments in the regulation of their domestic banking system. The core problem with banks and financial markets is their herd mentality and their short memories. During the first six months of 1997, international banks lent $32bn to Asia, most of it it the form of short-term loans. This was a 15 per cent increase over such lending in the last six months of 1996, despite clear signs of an impending crisis. It appears that, like the domestic banks in East Asia, the international financial community assumed that the high returns of the past would be continued indefinitely into the future. The same banks, under pressure from the US Treasury, are now being forced to reschedule loans to East Asia in an effort to avert a debt moratorium. Many of them had made the same mistake in lending to Latin America during the 1970s, and in purchasing Mexican treasury bills prior to the 1994–5 crisis. In both cases, they had to be bailed out by the US Treasury and the IMF.

As suggested earlier, the case for bailing out imprudent foreign lenders is weak, raising as it does problems of moral hazard. But the real challenge is to regulate domestic financial systems with a view to preventing their destabilisation. Lessons from international experience suggest that three elements are important:

- *Strict and effective regulation:* independent supervision of banks and a strong, independent central bank are needed to enforce rules on capital requirements, the valuation of assets, and disclosure of information on debt. In Chile, banks are forbidden by law to hold shares in companies or other banks. The need for effective surveillance of credit provision, especially in property markets, is critical for East Asia and other developing regions.[228]

- *Discouragement of short-term capital flows:* short-term surges of capital are inherently destabilising. Inflows have the effect of driving up the exchange rate (with potentially adverse implications for exports), while outflows exercise downward pressure on the national currency. The use of interest rates to contain market disruptions can have potentially damaging consequences for investment. There are several examples of successful policies to deter short-term private-capital flows. In 1993, Malaysia imposed a prohibition on the sale by domestic residents of short-term money-market instruments to foreigners in response to a surge in short-term capital inflows. Chile has a particularly effective record in regulating capital inflows, discouraging short-term speculative inflows into banking and equity markets through a transaction tax and a requirement that investors deposit 30 per cent of their funds with the Central Bank for one year for no interest payments.[229] It has also retained controls on capital outflows in the interest of exchange-rate stability.

- *Limits on foreign ownership and investment:* there are strong reasons for developing countries to insulate their financial systems from foreign control, not least to ensure that capital markets are geared towards the achievements of national development priorities. For instance, capital movements associated with foreign-owned banks could require major monetary and interest-rate adjustments, resulting in market instability.

One of the lessons to be leant from Chile's success is that strong regulation of the banking system is a prerequisite for financial stability.[230] The problem is that IMF conditionality is geared heavily towards capital-market liberalisation, with insufficient concern over the destabilising effects of short-term flows. Looking to the future, there is a danger that the Multilateral Agreement on Investment will provide this approach with legal enforcement, as governments are required to allow foreign investors the same rights in domestic capital-markets as their national counterparts. The blueprint is unwarranted and a potential threat to global financial stability.

At the international level East Asia's problems have highlighted the absence either of effective regulatory structures, or institutional arrangements for responding to crises as they emerge. The transformation of global markets has proceeded at a rapid pace, without the development of global financial institutions to supervise markets and report on capital flows. A formal institution with real authority is needed to fill this vacuum. Such an institution would need the political authority to demand full disclosure from public financial institutions and private markets. It would also need to establish standards for fund managers. Such standards are strictly enforced by authorities such as the US Securities Commission at a national level, but there is no international equivalent. This is needed to improve disclosure of risk in the interests both of developing countries, and of savers in the industrialised world whose assets are managed by pension and mutual funds.

Turning to the question of crisis management, the Group of Seven countries were persuaded by the Mexican crisis to make the IMF the global lender-of-last-resort. It was a bad choice. The IMF responded to the Mexican crisis by ensuring that foreign investors were repaid, while the costs of adjusting to the financial collapse were transferred to the poor in the form of reduced employment and lower public spending on health and education. The interests of Wall Street were given precedence over the needs of poor Mexicans. This followed the pattern of IMF debt-management in the 1980s, when repayments to commercial bank creditors were given priority over social and economic recovery. The danger now is that the Mexican 'rescue' model will be imposed on East Asia, with the interests of the poor sacrificed to those of foreign investors and speculators. What is needed is a more equitable approach to debt management, in which creditors absorb part of the costs of the debt crises to which they have contributed.

Notes

1   World Bank *Clear Water, Blue Skies: China's Environment in the new Century*. Washington 1997 pp17–20.

2   Ahuja V et al *Everyone's Miracle: Revisiting Poverty and Inequality in East Asia*. World Bank, Washington 1977 p6. Poverty headcount figures for China are highly sensitive to the poverty line chosen. This figure is based on the World Bank's poverty line of $1 a day at 1985 prices. The Chinese Government's national poverty line is around 40 per cent lower and reduces the numbers in poverty by 200 million. Unless stated all figures in this book use the $1 a day poverty line.

3   Greenfield G 'Everyone's state? Redefining an effective state in East Asia', Oxfam Hong Kong et al, mimeo, Hong Kong, 1997.

4   Bello W 'The end of the southeast Asian miracle', *Focus on the Global South*, Bangkok, mimeo, 1997; Lingle C *The Rise and Decline of the Asian Century*, Sirocco, Barcelona, 1997.

5   Brittain S 'Asian model, RIP', *Financial Times*, 4 December 1997.

6   *The Economist* 'Malaysia's misdiagnosis', 2 August 1997.

7   Sachs J 'Power unto itself', *Financial Times*, 11 December 1997.

8   Wolf M 'Same old IMF medicine', *Financial Times*, 10 December 1997.

9   *Financial Times* 'Korea's rescue', 10 December 1997.

10   Sen A 'Human rights and Asian values', *The New Republic* 14–21 July 1997, p33.

11   See, for example, World Bank *The East Asian Miracle: Economic Growth and Public Policy*, Oxford University Press, 1993; Krueger A, *Liberalisation Attempts and Consequences*, National Bureau of Economic Research, New York, 1987.

12   Stein H 'The World Bank, neo-classical economics and the application of Asian industrial policy to Africa', in Stein H (ed) *Asian Industrialisation and Africa: Studies in Policy Alternatives to Structural Adjustment*, Macmillan 1995.

13   There is now a large literature on this subject. For a good summary and overview see Mosley P and Week J 'Has recovery begun?

Africa's adjustment in the 1980s revisited', *World Development* 21:10, 1993.

14 World Bank, *World Development 1981*, Washington, p 21. For an example of the 'free market' interpretation of the Asian miracle see Balassa B, *The Newly Industrialised Countries in the World Economy*, Macmillan 1981; Little I, 'The experience and causes of rapid labour-intensive development in Korea, Taiawan, Hong Kong and Singapore', in Lee E (ed) *Export-led Industrialisation*, ILO, Geneva, 1981.

15 Wade R *Governing the Market: Economic Theory and the Role of Government in East Asia*, Princeton 1990.

16 Higgins B *Indonesia's Economic Stabilisation and Development*, Institute of Pacific relations, New York, 1975.

17 Myrdal G, *Asian Drama: An Inquiry into the Poverty of Nations*, Penguin, 1968, p489.

18 On trends in world poverty see United Nations Development Programme, *Human Development Report 1997*, New York Chs 1–2

19 World Summit for Social Development *Report of the World Summit for Social Development*, Copenhagen, 1995.

20 On the role of production in poverty alleviation see International Fund for Agricultural Development, *The State of the World Rural Poverty*, IFAD Rome 1992.

21 Alesina A and Rodrick D 'Distributive policies and economic growth', *Quarterly Journal of Economics* 109, May 1992, 465–490. On the adverse implications of poverty for economic growth see also Lipton M 'Growth and poverty reduction: which way round?' Background paper prepared for UNDP *Human Development Report 1997*, mimeo.

22 Bruton H *The Political Economy of Poverty, Equity and Growth: Sri Lanka and Malaysia*, Oxford University Press, 1992.

23 The poverty figures for East Asia are based on Ahuja V et al *Everyone's miracle*, op cit. Wider human welfare indicators in this section are drawn from UNDP *Human Development Report* (various years), Oxford University Press,; UNICEF *The State of the World's Children*, (various years) Oxford University Press; World Bank *World Development Indicators 1997*, Washington, 1997.

24 World Bank *Taking Action for Poverty Reduction in sub-Saharan Africa: Report of an African Region Task Force*, Washington 1996, p 5.

25 United Nations Development Programme *Human Development Report, 1997*, OUP, Oxford, 1997, page 72.

26 Birdsall N 'Inequality as a constraint on growth in Latin America'. In Turnham D (ed) *Social Tensions, Job Creation and Economic Policy in Latin America*, OECD, Paris 1995.

27   Maddison A *Monitoring the World Economy*, OECD, Paris 1995;
     Levine P *Is Asian Growth a Threat to the West?* University of Surrey,
     Department of Economics Working Paper 97:1, pp14–15.

28   The World Bank *China 2020: Development Challenges in the 21st
     Century*, Washington 1997, p1

29   ul Haq M *Human Development in South Asia*, OUP, Oxford 1997, p38.

30   Burki S 'Poverty returns in Pakistan', unpublished mimeograph,
     Human Development Centre, Islamabad 1996.

31   United Nation's Children's Fund (UNICEF) *The Progress of Nations*,
     New York, OUP, 1996. UNICEF *The State of the World's Children*,
     New York, OUP 1996. UNICEF *Challenges and Opportunities: Basic
     Education for All in Pakistan*, Report of a UN inter-agency mission
     on basic education, Islamabad, 1995.

32   UNDP *Human Development Report 1997*, op cit, pp74–75.

33   On the relationship between growth and distribution in sub-
     Saharan Africa see World Bank *Taking Action for Poverty Reduction in
     Sub-Saharan Africa*, op cit . pp18-19. See also Lipton M and Ravaillon
     M *Poverty and Policy*, Policy Research Working Paper No. 1130,
     Policy Research Department, World Bank, April, 1993.

34   Economic Commission for Latin America *The Equity Gap*,
     Santiago, April 1997

35   World Bank Global *Economic Prospects and the Developing Countries*,
     Chapter 1 and appendix 1 passim. Washington 1997.

36   Burki S 'Poverty returns in Pakistan', op cit.

37   World Bank *India: Achievements and Challenges in Reducing Poverty:
     a World Bank Country Study*, Washington 1997, pxiii.

38   Ahuja V et al, *Everyone's Miracle*, op. cit.

39   OECD *Adjustment and Equity in Malaysia*, Paris 1992.

40   On the New Economic Programme see Bruton H *The Political
     Economy of Poverty, Equity and Growth*, op cit.

41   Government of Malaysia *Poverty Eradication, Expansion of Productive
     Employment and Social Integration in Malaysia 1971–1994*, Kuala
     Lumpur 1995.

42   Birdsall N and Londono J *Asset Inequality Does Matter: Lessons from
     Latin America*, Inter-American Development Bank, Washington, 1997.

43   ibid

44   World Bank *Sharing Rising Incomes: Disparities in China*, Washington
     1997 p10

45   The theoretical underpinnings for this view originate with Kuznets
     S 'Economic growth and income inequality', *American Economic
     Review* 45:1, March 1955.

46 Such an approach figured prominently in the thinking of monetarist economists in the 1980s. A highly influential exposition of the same view for developing countries can be found three decades earlier in Galenson W and Leibenstein H 'Investment criteria, productivity and economic development', *Quarterly Journal of Economics* 80, 1955.

47 Birdsall N et al *Why Low Inequality Spurs Growth: Savings and Investment by the Poor*, Inter-American Development Bank, Washington, 1996.

48 IFAD *The State of World Rural Poverty*, IFAD, Rome, 1992, passim.

49 See, for example, Clarke G 'More evidence on income distribution and growth', *Journal of Development Economics*, 1995. Also Birdsall N et al 'Inequality and growth reconsidered', *World Bank Economic Review* 9.3 1995.

50 Deininger K and Squire L *Does Inequality Matter? Re-examining the Links between Growth and Inequality*, World Bank, Washington, 1996.

51 Scott C 'The distributive impact of the new economic model in Chile', in Bulmer-Thomas V (ed) *The New Economic Model in Latin America and its Impact on Income Distribution and Poverty*, Macmillan, 1996.

52 Birdsall N, Ross D and Sabot R 'Inequality as a constraint on growth in Latin America' in Turnham D et al *Social Tensions, Job Creation and Economic Policy in Latin America*, OECD, Paris 1995, pp178–9.

53 Kumar S 'Exit time from poverty', Background Paper prepared for the *Human Development Report*, mimeo, UNDP, 1997.

54 Aiguo L *Welfare Changes in China During the Economic Reforms*, World Institute for Development Economics Research (WIDER), Helsinki, 1996.

55 ul Haq *Human Development in South Asia*, 1997, p31.

56 UNDP *Human Development Report* op cit pp 49–50. On the relationship between growth and poverty reduction in India, see also Ravaillon M and Datt G 'India's chequered history in the fight against poverty: are there lessons for the future?' *Economic and Political Weekly* Vol. XXX1 1996.

57 Dreze J and Sen A *India: Economic Development and Social Opportunity*, OUP, Oxford 1995.

58 Shariff A 'Elementary education in India: differentials and determinants', National Council of Applied Economic Research, New Delhi, mimeo, 1996.

59 Ghayur S (ed) *South Asia: Employment Generation and Poverty Alleviation*, Friedrich Ebert Stiftung Institute, Islamabad. See also Human Rights Watch *The Small Hands of Slavery: Bonded Labour in India*, Washington, 1996.

60 Dreze J and Sen A *India: Economic Development and Social Opportunity*, op cit.

61 Loh J *Education and Economic Growth in India: An Aggregate Production Function Approach*, Ministry of Human Resource Development, New Delhi 1995.

62 World Bank *Sharing Rising Incomes: Disparities in China*, op cit, pp1–2.

63 ibid pp16–17

64 *The Economist* 'Inequality: for richer, for poorer', 5 November 1994.

65 Ahuja V *Everyone's Miracle*, op cit, p42

66 Birdsall N, Ross D and Sabot R 'Inequality and growth reconsidered', *The World Bank Economic Review* 9:3, September 1995.

67 Deininger K and Squire L *Does Inequality Matter?* op. cit.

68 Birdsall N and Londoro J *Asset Inequality Does Matter*, op cit.

69 Economic Commission for Latin America 'The equity gap', Paper presented to the First Regional Conference in Follow-up to the World Summit for Social Development, Sao Paulo, April 1997.

70 ibid.

71 United Nations Education, Social and Cultural Organisation *Statistical Yearbook*, New York 1973.

72 Birdsall N and Sabot R *Opportunities Forgone: Education, Growth and Inequality in Brazil*, Inter-American Development Bank, Washington, 1995. See also Behrman J *The Action of Human Resources and Poverty on Each Other: What we have Yet to Learn*, World Bank LSMS Working Paper 74, 1996.

73 Jones G and Hall T *Indonesia Assessment: Population and Human Resources*, Australian National University, 1996, Chapter 8.

74 ibid.

75 On education in Indonesia See Hill H *The Indonesian Economy since 1966* op cit, pp206–213.

76 Booth A 'Rapid economic growth and poverty decline: a comparison of Indonesia and Thailand', *Journal of International Development* 9:2, 1997, p 170–172.

77 ibid, pp182–183.

78 Carrin G et al *The Reform of the Co-operative Medical System in the People's Republic of China*, World Health Organisation, Macro-economics, Health and Development Series, 1996.

79 United Nations Childrens Fund *Catching Up: Capacity Development for Poverty Alleviation in Vietnam*, Hanoi, 1995, p78.

80 Fritzen S *Situation Analysis and Capacity Development Issues for Basic Health in Vietnam*, UNDP, Hanoi 1996.

81 Tipping G et al *Quality of Public Health Services and Household Health-care Decisions in Rural Communes of Vietnam*, IDS Research Report 27, 1994.

82 Witter S 'Rural health services in China: their relevance for Vietnam', *IDS Bulletin* 28:1, 1997.

83 ibid.

84 Zhang A 'Poverty alleviation in China: commitment, policies and expenditure'. Background paper for the 1997 *Human Development Report*, UNDP, Oxford University Press.

85 Aiguo L *Welfare Changes in China During the Economic Reforms*, WIDER, Helsinki, 1996, p41.

86 Zhang A 'Poverty alleviation in China' op cit.

87 Tang S et al *Financing Health Services in China: Adapting to Economic Reform*, IDS Research Report 26, Brighton, 1996.

88 World Bank *China 2020: Development Challenges in the new Century* op cit., p55.

89 World Bank *Financing Health Care: Issues and Options for China*, Washington 1997.

90 Carrin G 'Reforming the rural cooperative medical system in China', *IDS Bulletin* 28.1 1997.

91 World Bank *Financing Health Care: Issues and Options for China*, op cit.

92 ibid.

93 ibid.

94 Hao Y et al 'Equity in the utilisation of medical services: a survey in poor rural China', *IDS Bulletin* 28:1, 1997.

95 Zhang C 'The co-operative medical care system in Yuhan County' in Gu X et al (ed) *Study of Health Care Financing System in Rural China*, Shanghai Science and Technology Press, Shanghai, 1991. On cost as a barrier to health services see also Gu X and Yu H 'Farmers' expenditure on basic medical care: a study in poor rural areas', *Chinese Primary Health Care* 8, 1994, pp21–23.

96 Aiguo L *Welfare Changes in China During the Economic Reforms*, op cit.

97 World Bank *China 2020: Development Challenges in the new Century* op cit . p 54. On evidence of a deterioration in human welfare indicators, see also Aiguo L, op. cit.

98 Bogg L et al 'The cost of coverage: rural health insurance in China', in *Health Policy and Planning* 11:3, 1995, pp238–252. See also Henderson G et al 'Equality and the utilisation of health services: report of an eight-province survey in China', in *Social Science and Medicine*, 39:5, 1996, pp687–699.

99 World Bank *Financing Health Care: Issues and Options for China*, op cit.

100 World Bank *Vietnam Poverty Assessment and Strategy*, Washington 1995.

101 United Nations *Poverty Alleviation in Vietnam*, UNICEF/UNDP, Hanoi, 1995.

102 Oxfam GB 'Report on financing and delivery of basic services at the commune level in Ky Anh, Ha Tinh, Vietnam', Hanoi, March 1996.

103 World Bank *Vietnam: Fiscal Decentralisation and the Delivery of Rural Services*, Wshington 1996, p38.

104 Ensor T and San P 'Access and payment for health care: the poor of northern Vietnam', *International Journal of Health Planning and Management* 11, pp69–83, 1996.

105 On the interaction between health costs and livelihoods for the poor see Russel S 'Ability to pay for health care: concepts and evidence', *Health Policy and Planning* 11:3, 1996, pp219–237.

106 Fritzen S *Situation Analysis and Capacity Development Issues for Basic Health in Vietnam*, op cit, pp40–43. See also Donovan D (ed) *Development Trends in Vietnam's Northern Mountain Regions*, Centre for Natural Resources and Environmental Studies, Vietnam National University, Hanoi, 1997; ADUKI *Poverty in Vietnam: A Report for the Swedish International Development Agency*, Hanoi, April 1995; UNICEF *Catching Up*, op cit.

107 World Bank *Vietnam Poverty Assessment and Strategy*, Washington 1995.

108 Gertler P and Litvak J 'Health care during transition: the role of the private sector in Vietnam', in Dollar D et al (ed) *Household Welfare and Vietnam's Transition to a Market Economy*, World Bank, 1996.

109 World Bank *A Strategy to Fight Poverty: the Philippines*, Country Operations Division, Washington 1995, Chapter 4.

110 UNDP *The Philippinines Human Development Report*, Manila 1995.

111 Freedom from Debt Coalition 'Health and adjustment in the Philippines', mimeo, Manila 1995.

112 World Bank *Cost and Financing Issues in Education*, Poverty and Social Policy Department report, Washington 1995.

113 Birdsall N and Sabot R *Opportunities Forgone: Education, Growth and Inequality in Brazil*. Inter-American Development Bank, Washington, 1996. See also Psacharopolous G and Ng Y 'Earnings and education in Latin America', *Education Economics* 2:2, 1994.

114 Jones C and Kiguel M *Adjustment in Africa: Reform, Results and the Road Ahead*, World Bank, 1994.

115 Oxfam GB *Oxfam Poverty Report*, Oxford 1996.

116 The following section is based on figures from UNDP *Human Development Report, 1997*, op. cit.; UNICEF *The State of the World's Children*, 1995, op. cit.; World Bank *Social Indicators*, 1996, op. cit.

117 This section draws on the Inter-American Development Bank *Economic and Social Progress in Latin America: Making Social Services Work*, Washington 1996, Part 3 Chapter 2.

118 Morley S and Silva A *Problems and Performance in Primary Education: Why do Systems Differ?* Inter-American Development Bank, Washington, 1994.

119 Inter-American Development Bank *Economic and Social Indicators*, op. cit.

120 World Bank *Country Assistance Strategy for Brazil*, Washington, April, 1997.

121 Krishnan T 'Access to health and burden of treatment in India: an inter-state comparison', Centre for Development Economics, Delhi School of Economics, mimeo, 1996, New Delhi. See also Harriss J et al *Economic Reform in India: Potential Impact on Poverty Reduction and Implications for Social Policy*, London School of Economics, Development Studies Institute, December 1992.

122 Dreze J and Sen A *India: Economic Development and Social Opportunity*, op cit, p 39.

123 UNESCO *World Education Report 1995*, Oxford, 1996. On the state of education in Africa, see also Appleton, S et al, 'Education and health in sub-Saharan Africa', *Journal of International Development* 8:3, 1996.

124 Government of Uganda *Equity and Vulnerability: A Situation Analysis of Women, Adolescents and Children in Uganda*, 1994, Kampala, Chapter 4.

125 Government of Uganda *A Poverty Eradication Action Plan for Uganda* Volume 1, Kampala, 1996, p84.

126 Oxfam GB 'Poor country debt relief: false dawn or new hope for poverty reduction', April 1996.

127 Government of Uganda *Background to the Budget 1997/1998*, Kampala, p80.

128 Harvard Institute for International Development *Repetition in Primary Schools in Honduras*, Cambridge Mass, 1992.

129 Inter-American Development Bank *Economic and Social Progress in Latin America: Making Social Services Work*, op cit p 279.

130 Sahn D 'Public expenditures in sub-Saharan Africa during a period of economic reforms', *World Development*, 20, 1992. See also World Bank *The Social Impact of Adjustment Operations: An Overview*, Operations Evaluation Department, 1995, p102.

131 For evidence of public spending cuts under structural adjustment see Oxfam GB *Oxfam Poverty Report*, op cit, Chapter 4.
132 World Bank *India: New Directions in Health Sector Development at the State Level, an Operational Perspective*, Washington, 1997
133 World Bank *Zambia: Poverty Assessment* Vol 1, Washington, 1994.
134 See, for example, Russel S *Ability to Pay for Health Care*, op cit.
135 For example, World Bank *The Poor and Cost Sharing in the Social Sectors of Sub-Saharan Africa*, Washington 1995 proposes a high level of caution in adopting user-fee strategies. By contrast, operational documents often strongly endorse cost-recovery at all levels. An example is the World Bank's 1994 'District health service pilot and demonstration project for Uganda', East Africa Department, Washington 1994.
136 Booth D 'Coping with cost recovery'. Report to the Swedish International Development Authority, Stockholm University, 1995.
137 Lennock J *Paying for Health: Poverty and Structural Adjustment in Zimbabwe*, Oxfam GB 1994.
138 Mwabu G et al 'User charges in Government health facilities in Kenya: effect on attendance and revenue, *Health Policy and Planning* 10:2, 1993.
139 World Bank *China 2020: Development Challenges in the New Century*, op cit, p16.
140 World Bank *Country Assistance Strategy for Brazil*, op cit, p 7.
141 World Bank 'Uganda: public spending tracking survey', mimeo, Washington 1996.
142 UNDP *Human Development Report 1997*, op cit.
143 Based on universal primary education costing figures in World Bank *Primary Education in India*, Washington 1997, and military spending figures in UNDP *Human Development Report 1997*, op cit.
144 Government of Uganda *Background to the Budget 1997*, op cit, p80.
145 World Bank *India: Achievements and Challenges in Reducing Poverty*, op cit, p 21.
146 Inter-American Development Bank *Economic and Social Progress in Latin America*, op cit, p128.
147 Davies R 'Assessing the causes and sustainability of the budget deficit', University of Harare, Department of Economics, mimeo, 1996.
148 On Mozambique's debt problems see Oxfam International 'Debt relief for Mozambique: investing in peace', August 1997.
149 For a critical appraisal of the Highly Indebted Poor Countries initiative see Oxfam International 'Poor country debt relief', April 1997.

150 OECD *Development Assistance Committee Report 1996*, Paris, 1996, p94.

151 ibid, Table 27.

152 On this theme see Cairns E *A Safer Future: Reducing the Human Cost of War*, Oxfam GB, 1997.

153 World Bank *The East Asian Miracle: Economic Growth and Public Policy*, op cit. The same line of argument is advanced annually in the World Bank's *Global Economic Prospects and the Developing Countries*. For a standard presentation of the view that East Asia's success was free-market driven, see Ranis G and Mahmood S *The Political Economy of Development Policy Change*, Blackwell, Oxford 1992. The most influential economist in popularising the shortcoming of interventionist policies aimed at import-substitution is Anne Krueger. See Krueger A *Political Economy of Policy Reform in Developing Countries*, MIT Press 1993.

154 For example, Stein H 'The World Bank and the application of Asian industrial policy to Africa', *Journal of International Development*, May/June 1994.

155 On the distinction between micro-economic policies and macro-economic disequilibrium see Rodrik D 'Understanding economic policy reform', *Journal of Economic Literature*, XXX1V, 1996, pp9–41.

156 United Nations Conference on Trade and Development *Trade and Development Report 1997*, Geneva, p 85.

157 World Bank *Global Economic Prospects 1996*, Washington, 1996.

158 United Nations Conference on Trade and Development *The Least Developed Countries 1996 Report*, New York and Geneva, p44.

159 World Bank *Global Development Finance*, Washington 1997, Chapter 2.

160 Griffiths Jones S et al *Latin American and Asian Perspectives on Managing Capital Surges*, World Institute for Development Economics Research, Helsinki, mimeo, 1997.

161 On the weak relationship between growth and employment in Latin America see Buendia H 'The elusive miracle: Latin America in the 1990s', World Institute for Development Economics Research, *World Development Studies* 9, March 1996, Helsinki.

162 On poverty in employment in Chile see Diaz A *Restructuring and the Working Classes in Chile*, United Nations Research Institute for Social Development, Geneva, 1993.

163 Fitzgerald E 'The new trade regime, macro-economic behaviour and income distribution in Latin America' in Bulmer-Thomas V (ed) *The New Economic Model in Latin America and its Impact on Income Distribution and Poverty*, Macmillan, 1996.

164 The following account of industrial policy in East Asia draws on: Lall S 'Technological capabilities and industrialisation', *World Development*

20:2, London 1992; Lall S *Industrial Policy: The Role of Government in Promoting Industrial and Technology Development*, UNCTAD, Geneva, 1994; Amsden A *Asia's Next Giant: South Korea and Late Industrialisation*, Oxford University Press, 1989; Wade R *Governing the Market: Economic Theory and the Role of Government in East Asia*, Princeton University Press, 1990; Hill H *The Indonesian Economy since 1966*, op cit.

165 Sachs J 'The myth of Asia's miracle', *Foreign Affairs* 736, 1997.

166 World Bank *Global Development Finance 1997*, Washington, 1997.

167 On agrarian reform in East Asia see Griffin K *The Political Economy of Agrarian Change*, London, Macmillan 1974; Fei J et al *Growth and Equity: The Taiwan Case*, Oxford University Press 1979; Song B *The Rise of the Korean Economy*, Oxford University Press 1990; McKinley T 'The distribution of wealth in rural China', in Griffin K and Renwei Z (ed) *The Distribution of Income in China*, Macmillan 1993.

168 Binswanger H et al 'Power, distortions, revolt and reform in agricultural land relations' in Behrman J and Srinivasan T (ed) *Handbook of Development Economics* Vol 111, North Holland, Amsterdam, 1995. See also UNDP *Human Development Report 1997*, op cit, pp74–75.

169 High levels of inequality in the distribution of assets has been identified as one of the most powerful brakes on growth. See, for example, Deninger K and Squire L *Does Inequality Matter?* op cit; See also Birdsall N and Londono J *Asset inequality does matter*, op cit

170 UNDP *Human Development Report 1996*, op cit.

171 Binswanger H 'The policy response of agriculture', *Supplement to the World Policy Economic Review and World Bank Research Observer*, World Bank, Washington 1989.

172 Lipton M and Maxwell S *The New Poverty Agenda: An Overview* Institute of Development Studies, Discussion Paper 306, 1992. See also Lipton M 'How economic growth affects poverty', background Paper for UNDP *Human Development Report 1997*.

173 Lipton M 'Land reform as unfinished business: the evidence against stopping', *World Development* 21:4, April 1993. See also Griffin K and McKinley T *Implementing a Human Development Strategy*, Macmillan 1994, pp81–83.

174 See Morley S *Poverty and Inequality in Latin America: The Impact of Adjustment and Recovery in the the 1980s*, John Hopkins University Press, Baltimore 1995. On land struggles in Brazil, see *The Economist* 'Land in Brazil', 13 April 1996.

175 On the Gini coefficient for land ownership in China see Deininger K and Squire L 'A new data set for measuring income inequality', *The World Bank Economic Review* 10:3, 1996.

176 McMillan J et al 'The impact of China's economic reforms on agricultural productivity growth', *Journal of Political Economy*, 97, 1989.

177 UNDP/UNICEF *Catching Up: Capacity Development for Poverty Elimination in Vietnam*, op cit.

178 On the slow pace of agrarian reform in The Philippines Balisacan A *Rural Poverty and Access to Land*, World Bank, Country Operations Division, Washington 1995.

179 On West Bengal see Sengupta S and Gazdar H 'Agrarian politics and rural development in West Bengal', in Dreze J and Sen A (ed) *Indian Development: Selected Regional Perspectives*, OUP, 1996.

180 Moyo S *The Land Question in Zimbabwe*, SAPES Books, Harare, 1995.

181 World Bank *Zimbabwe Country Economic Memorandum: Agricultural Sector*, Washington 1987.

182 Jayne T S et al 'Unravelling Zimbabwe's food insecurity paradox: implications for grain marketing reforms' in Jayne T S et al (ed) 'Integrating food and nutrition policy in Zimbabwe', University of Zimbabwe, mimeo, 1990.

183 World Bank *Understanding Poverty in Zimbabwe: Changes in the 1990s and Directions for the Future*, Washington, 1996.

184 World Bank *Zimbabwe: Achieving Shared Growth*, Country Economic Memorandum, Washington 1995, p97.

185 Hill H *The Indonesian Economy since 1966*, op cit, p 123.

186 On the operation of the BULOG see Ellis F 'The rice market and its management in Indonesia', *IDS Bulletin* 21:3, 1990.

187 Booth A *Rapid Economic Growth and Poverty Decline: A Comparison of Indonesia and Thailand 1981–1990*, op cit.

188 On the creation of food dependence in Nigeria see Beckman B and Andrea G *The Wheat Trap: Bread and Underdevelopment in Nigeria*, Zed, 1985. For a wider view, see Raikes P *Modernising Hunger*, CIIR, London, 1988. For a more recent analysis of the way in which export subsidisation undermines local food markets and cultivates dependence on imports see Watkins K, 'Farm fallacies', *The Ecologist* 26:6, December 1996.

189 On the extent of food import dependence in low-income countries see FAO *The State of Food and Agriculture 1996*, Rome 1996.

190 Appendini K 'Agriculture and farmers within NAFTA: a Mexican perspective' in Bulmer Thomas V *Mexico and the North America Free Trade Agreement: Who Will Benefit*, Macmillan, 1994.

191 Oxfam GB 'Trade liberalisation as a threat to livelihoods', December, 1996. On the implications for poverty in the main corn producing areas see Alternative Forum for Research in Mindanao, *The Poverty Situation in Mindanao*, Davao, 1994.

192 Appendini K 'Agriculture and farmers within NAFTA', op cit.

193 OECD *Agricultural Policies, Markets and Trade in OECD Countries*, Paris, 1996.

194 UNDP *Human Development Report 1997*, op cit, p38.

195 Johnson S and Rogaly B *Micro-finance and Poverty Reduction*, Oxfam Development Guidelines, Oxfam GB 1997, pp 10–12.

196 ibid, pp85–96.

197 Goetz A and Sen Gupta R 'Who takes the credit? Gender, power and control over loan use in rural credit programmes in Bangladesh', *World Development* 24:1, 1994.

198 Robinson M 'Savings mobilisation and micro-enterprise finance: the Indonesian experience' in Otero M and Rhyne E (ed) *The New World of Micro-enterprise Finance*, Intermediate Technology Publications, London, 1994.

199 World Bank *Global Economic Prospects and the Developing Countries 1997*, op cit, p 11. See also *The Economist* 'The Asian miracle: is it over?' 1 March 1997.

200 Montagnon P 'Asian tigers catch a virus', *Financial Times* 17 July 1997.

201 Ridding J and Kynge J 'Complacency gives way to contagion', *Financial Times* 13 January 1998.

202 *The Economist* 'Thailand gets the bill', 9 August 1997.

203 Sander T 'IMF aims at budget but not private debt', *Financial Times* 18 January 1998.

204 *Financial Times* 'A threat to the world... and also to South Korea', 20 November 1997.

205 *The Economist* 'The Chaebol drag each other down', 13 December 1997.

206 Bardacke T 'The day the miracle came to an end', *Financial Times* 12 January 1998.

207 *Economic Outlook*, second half of 1997, OECD, Paris.

208 *The Economist* 'The IMF's struggle in East Asia', 13 December 1997, p.95.

209 Sources for the section on the Mexican economic crisis: Castaneda J 'Mexico's circle of misery', *Foreign Affairs*, New York, July/August 1996; Griffith-Jones S *Causes and Lessons of the Mexican Peson Peso Crisis*, World Institute for Development Economics Research, Working Paper, Helsinki, 1996; UNDP *Human Development Report 1997*, op cit, p 88.

210 The conditions attached to IMF loans to East Asia have not been published. Reported details can be found in Burton J 'Painful prospect', *Financial Times* 8 December 1997; Fidler S 'Might Asia lose a decade?', *Financial Times*, 27 November 1997; Wolf M 'The same old IMF medicine', *Financial Times* 17 November 1997; *The Economist* 'What the doctor ordered', 9 August 1997; *Business Week*

'Another year of living dangerously' 8 December 1997; Sachs J 'Power unto itself' *Financial Times*, 11 December 1997; *Financial Times* 'Korea's rescue' 15 November 1997.

211 Wolf M 'The same old IMF medicine', op cit.

212 *Far Eastern Economic Economic Review* 'End of the line', 22 January 1998.

213 Wolf M 'The same old IMF medicine' op. cit; *The Economist* 'New illness, same old medicine', 13 December, 1997; Sachs J 'Power unto itself' op. cit.

214 Fischer S 'IMF: the right stuff', *Financial Times* 17 December 1997.

215 Veneroso F and Wade R *The Asian Financial Crisis*, Brown University, 1998.

216 *The Economist* 'Asia's economic crisis', 15 November 1997, p.26.

217 Wolf M 'Caging the bankers', *Financial Times* 20 January 1998.

218 Montagnon P and Thoenes S 'On the critical list', *Financial Times* 16 January 1998.

219 *Financial Times* 'High risk in Korea', 11 December 1997.

220 *The Economist* 'Meanwhile, back where the wagons are circling', 29 November 1997. See also *Business Week* 'Another year of living dangerously'; *Far Eastern Economic Review* 'Now's your chance', 11 September 1997.

221 Wolfensohn J 'Asia: the long view', *Financial Times* 29 January 1998.

222 Fitzgerald E 'Intervention versus regulation: the role of the IMF in crisis prevention and management', UNCTAD, Geneva, mimeo, April 1996.

223 Soros G 'Capital crimes', *Atlantic Monthly*, January, 1997.

224 Soros G 'Avoiding a breakdown', *Financial Times* 31 December 1997.

225 Reich R 'Deflation: the real enemy', *Financial Times* 15 January 1998.

226 Cited in *Financial Times* 13 January 1998.

227 Felix D 'Financial globalisation versus free trade: the case for the Tobin tax', *UNCTAD Bulletin*, January-February 1996, Geneva.

228 For a good account of the regulatory devices available to governments see Sta Ana F 'Holding a brief for bolder intervention in regulating capital flows', Action for Economic Reforms, Manila, mimeo, July 1997.

229 Griffiths Jones S et al *Latin American and Asian Perspectives on Managing Capital Surges*, WIDER op cit.

230 Fidler S 'Lessons form Chile for crisis in Asia', *Financial Times* 14 January 1998.